THE BODY LANGUAGE

to all the players, officials and supporters
of Tottenham Hotspur, 1967 to whenever, for all the
pleasures,
problems, possibilities....

THE BODY LANGUAGE

the meaning of modern sport

ANDREW BLAKE

LAWRENCE & WISHART
LONDON

Lawrence & Wishart Limited
99A Wallis Road
London E9 5LN

First published 1996

British Library Cataloguing in Publication Data
A catalogue record for this book is available from the British Library.

ISBN 0 85315 834 7

Photoset in North Wales by
Derek Doyle & Associates, Mold, Flintshire.
Printed in Great Britain by
Redwood Books, Trowbridge.

Contents

Preface

As the 1995 Rugby Union World Cup, won in a blaze of emotion by the host nation, South Africa, was fading into memory, it was announced that the television magnate Rupert Murdoch had bought the other rugby code, Rugby League, in its entirety. The worldwide professional game would be restructured to accommodate new competitions; seasons would be changed to play the game on warmer and longer days, to give television coverage more predictability and crowds fewer blisters. A few weeks later, world rugby union officials announced that their game would officially turn professional. They too discussed the meaning of life with Mr Murdoch, and decided that it was principally about money; he signed up the southern hemisphere teams for ten years' worth of championships. Though these are still to be based on the national allegiances which have been part of the world of professional sport for the last 120 years, the clearly dominant force here is transnational television. Sport, once (behind warfare) the supreme carrier of national values, now carries audiences and advertising across national boundaries. In fronting global satellite television, sport will unquestionably change the values, the meaning, of 'nation'.

British Prime Minister John Major, meanwhile, was using money from the new national sport – gambling on the national lottery – to fund national schools of coaching excellence aimed at worldwide sporting success for British representative teams. Given Murdoch's global empire, and the fast-dissolving sense of national identity in Britain, this seems a typically Canute-like gesture from a sports fan of a certain age, who was youngish when Surrey regularly won

7

the county cricket championship and there were people there to watch them do it. Memory is a massively important part of sport, and memory drives the fantasy of future success; but memory fades all too quickly into nostalgia for a better past. What is needed is not to replicate the past, but to create a better sporting future. For all the limitations of his profit-driven vision, at least Murdoch is attempting this.

There is, in fact, one unfading memory from the 1995 rugby world cup – precisely because it is not so much a memory as a portent. A New Man appeared. The sight of the New Zealand wing, Jonah Lomu, seven feet tall and with thighs the width of mature trees, brushing aside opponents in order to score, and even more impressively accelerating from a standing start in order to do so, signals one of the most important ways in which sport has contributed to changing public consciousness. Sport has changed the body: our ideas about it, our fantasies and desires about its perfect form, of what it could and should be able to do. Important though the performing arts have been and remain in the public presentation of the body, sport is the pre-eminent language through which the body speaks; to men in particular, sport speaks the body more eloquently than any other form of human endeavour.

The connected essays in this book explore these propositions and relationships. Looking at the past and present through eyes informed by cultural theory but wary of its resistance to the world of sport, I try first to connect the two, asking what sport can mean to cultural studies and its analysis of popular culture. The rest of the book then builds on these connections, as I discuss the historical and geographical connections between sport and nation, and current concerns about design and the body, the performer and the participant, and finally sporting pleasures, always with an eye on the past – and the future – of this massive area of human activity.

I am grateful to everyone who has discussed sport, attended sporting events, or shouted at the television with me or against me over the years; special thanks to my brother, David Blake, and my father, Arthur Blake. Prakash Moolgavkar provided some interesting medical information, and introduced me to the relatively guilt-free country sport of clay pigeon shooting. Several people looked over versions of the manuscript and made pertinent comments – thanks to John Izod, Richard Reynolds and Candida Yates, and to Ruth Borthwick at Lawrence and Wishart. My colleagues in the Department of Cultural Studies at the University of East London allowed me time to develop this project; as always, they, and our students, have been a pleasure to work with even in the age of Mickey Mouse 'higher' education. I am very grateful to Christina Purcell and Matthew Bourke, whose hospitality allowed me to finish the manuscript in pleasant surroundings.

1 Sport in Culture, Sport in Cultural Studies

To begin with a mystery, which will be investigated as the book proceeds. The body of sport lies, not dead but virtually invisible, in the rapidly growing library which is the world of cultural studies. This relative invisibility is puzzling: cultural studies is above all concerned with popular culture, and sport is very much part of popular culture. Many people participate in it, either as amateurs or professionals, and many people observe it as spectators inside stadia, or by listening to the radio or watching television. At any rate, sport is continuously visible elsewhere in the world. Indeed, as this book will argue, sport is a crucial component of contemporary society, one very important way through which many of us understand our bodies, our minds, and the rest of the world.

This is true not only because of mass participation and observation: sport saturates the language that surrounds us. Sporting activity is reported in every newspaper; it forms an important part of the wider literary culture of magazines and books. Take the annual American journal of record, the *Britannica Yearbook* for 1994. In the section devoted to reviewing the previous year's events, 'Sports and Games' forms by far the longest entry. Forty pages are devoted to reports of events from the world of sport, and a further twenty-eight pages give 'the sporting record' of performance statistics (winners, newly broken records, times and distances); both national and global events are covered, from archery through gymnastics and rodeo to wrestling. By contrast, there are only twenty pages on

11

economic affairs, and coverage of the arts is far thinner, with only four pages each on dance, music (covering both classical and popular) and publishing.

Sport is also perpetually audible and visible through the electronic media. Television and radio devote a great deal of time to sport. There are whole departments of most networks devoted to sport as current affairs, providing everything from the brief reporting of results on news programmes to the saturation coverage of events like the Olympics, World Cups and national championships in team sports on both mainstream and dedicated programmes and channels. Sport is arguably one of the most powerful presences within broadcasting. Both on television and radio, the principle of live coverage is often taken to mean that sporting events have priority over others. As well as driving other programming from the screen at certain times of the year, sport can instantly reshape television in a way which can only be matched by political crises, or disasters involving loss of life. Unexpectedly rearranged fixtures, or more routinely, late finishing matches, disrupt published broadcast schedules, to the distress of people who do not wish to stay up late, or people who have programmed their video recorders to record scheduled programmes. This prioritised saturation coverage means that even those uninterested in sport, or hostile to it, cannot escape its nagging presence, as an ongoing part of the 'background noise' of contemporary culture.

It is precisely this background noise which cultural studies hopes to analyse, showing how the 'common sense', the ordinary, is constructed, and showing how we can read this common sense critically. Furthermore it is the cultural studies approach which has finally made the study of popular culture acceptable within the academic curriculum; and yet the presentation of a book on sport as a cultural studies text – which this book is, unashamedly – remains unusual. The mystery remains: the investigation must begin.

Cultural Studies is now a mature area of academic work; but it is not a 'discipline' in the same sense as other studies in the humanities like history and geography. This is deliberate. It was founded on the premise that these disciplinary boundaries should not just be crossed, but dismantled and recombined where possible, and it has fostered and encouraged a new set of ways of seeing and understanding the world. Using methods drawn from history, sociology, literary and film theory, feminist studies and psychoanalysis, cultural studies has pioneered the study of popular culture and furthered the critical revaluation of high culture. One of the most common forms of analysis adopted by people working in cultural studies is *deconstruction*. Very simply, this is the idea that critical analysis should reveal the gaps and absences in any cultural product, and that these absences tell us as much about the product as what it actually contains. Well, to deconstruct cultural studies for a moment . . . sport is one prominent absence from the roster of activities normally considered by cultural studies work. The notion of 'popular culture' adopted by cultural studies focuses in the main on media production and related activity such as music, and has continued to marginalise sporting activity. What does this tell us about cultural studies as it seeks for the meanings of contemporary culture?

In marginalising sport, cultural studies is in fact following the established patterns of academic study. Sport was long a problem for academic criticism both from the left and from the traditional humanities subjects such as literature and history. Generally the left simply dismissed it: some saw sport as a frivolous diversion from the real world of politics, something which was not actually harmful in itself, but wasn't part of the serious business of life. At worst it prevented people from giving their attention to politics. Others, however, claimed that it was an active colluder in the existing system, acting as an 'opiate of the people' to dull senses which would otherwise have been sensitive to their misfortune. It was argued that sport, like other aspects of 'mass' culture which attracted the disapproval of the left – Hollywood cinema, for instance – functioned to convey misleading messages about the world, in an attempt to make people believe in, and continue to act in, the existing power structure. In this argument sport formed part of a 'dominant ideology' which gave people who believed in it a 'false consciousness' about themselves and their place in the world. Sport could, for instance, tell people about the necessity of hard work, or team discipline: beliefs which are not natural aspects of the human condition, but which are useful in almost any political system, and which, the left argued, were especially useful to industrial capitalism.

Criticism from the left, of sport as of everything else, tended to target the western world's political and economic system. Capitalism and sport are of course closely intertwined in many parts of the world. As with most forms of pleasurable activity, sport in western societies usually involves buying and selling: from match tickets or television channel subscriptions for the observer, to clothing and equipment for the participant. Even aspects of the sporting process which appear to be outside this system of exchange – say a newspaper report on the early rounds of a tennis tournament – will often stand as an advertisement for the game in general and the tournament in particular, enticing the spectator to buy tickets or to view the remainder of the contest on television. At present almost all sport is, in other words, part of the system of the ownership and exchange of goods and services known as capitalism. It is possible to plot the history of sport as a gradual move towards this situation from a pre-capitalist world, in which participation or spectatorship did not involve capitalist exchanges. Therefore it was all too easy to see sport as a component of the capitalist system of class oppression, to denigrate its emphasis on competition, and even to assume that in a perfect world it would cease to exist. Sociologists and historians tended firstly to ignore sport; then, when from the mid-1960s they began to consider it, they saw it within these frameworks as either unimportant leisure practices or as harmful economic or ideological aspects of the class system.

One influential work in the latter category was the introduction, by social historians Eileen and Stephen Yeo, to a book they edited together called *Popular Culture and Class Conflict*.[1] Contemporary sport, they claimed, was an analogue of competitive, aggressive and destructive capitalism, both in its practices and in its organisational structures. Like all other leisure facilities and practices, it was owned and run by, and in the interests of, capitalism.

It divided the working class which might otherwise have been united against capitalism (dividing people into successful and unsuccessful sportsplayers, or into groups of mutually hostile supporters of different teams, for example) and it also took their money and time, which could have been spent in better ways. The Yeos' patronising, critical ideology of fear and loathing obviously left no place for the consideration of the pleasures of sport, and very little for the detailed analyses of its meanings. The 'meaning' was simply, and in this view unarguably, a consequence of its place within capitalism. It was not just an academic message. Many teachers had taken this structure of belief to heart in the 1970s, and began to refuse to teach competitive sport at schools, claiming in a more socially acceptable version of the anti-capitalist view, that as it produced losers as well as winners it was socially divisive. It is quite possible that this refusal to teach winners has made British sport into a consistent loser: recent failures of English, Welsh and Scottish soccer teams to qualify for the 1994 World Cup finals have been laid at the door of this policy of equality by default. No-one can compete, the argument goes, so no-one learns how to lose – or to win. The battle for the 1994 World Cup was lost on the egalitarian playing fields of Slough Comprehensive School.

Cultural Studies has thankfully questioned the naive assumptions behind this attempt to promote equality through anti-competitive practice, and has opened up debates in which meaning and pleasure become available to observers and participants, and pleasurable activities are not seen as merely the inevitable, and harmful, reflection of an economic structure. Given the complexity of analysis offered by recent work on identity, sexuality, and ethnicity, it is no longer convincing to divide the world simply into classes, and it is increasingly acceptable to see pleasures positively, as ways in which people forge and reaffirm their own identities. This has been one reason for the increasing attention given to many aspects of popular culture, in which cultural studies has attacked the divisions between 'high' and 'low' culture as they were taken to apply to literary texts, art and music in the study of the humanities. This critique of another socially divisive belief,

elitist aesthetics, has brought film and television into the
frame of serious study, and applied literary analysis to
popular texts – even in university departments of
literature. Similarly, the study of the techniques and
practices of popular music have become acceptable in
music studies from GCSE to degree level. The scope of the
humanities has been broadened.

But it has never been easy to see the study of sport as
part of the humanities. History has only recently begun to
consider sport. Even in the pioneering days of 'social
history', sport was virtually invisible in historical investigation; while there were plenty of histories of individual
sports written by enthusiasts, these were not intended to
offer contextual explanations of sport, but merely to tell
other enthusiasts what had happened within the various
competitions. Professional historians tended, like sociologists, to dismiss sports as frivolous activities without deep
meaning for their participants. Since the early 1970s,
pioneering work by people like Tony Mason and Wray
Vamplew, and the founding of the *International Journal for
the History of Sport*, have led to a massive increase in the
historical investigation of all sports.[2] While this work is
more contextually aware, and has produced valuable
insights (into, for example, the relationship between sport
and colonialism; or suburban sport, the domestic sphere,
and the role of women), there remains a reluctance for
historians to use the theoretical insights available to other
branches of the humanities. A few sociologists, on the
other hand, have produced fascinating studies of sport
which incorporate historical narrative with illuminating
theoretical insights into the ways in which sport works
within societies and individuals. The work of Allen
Guttmann, Jennifer Hargreaves, Ellis Cashmore, Norbert
Elias and Eric Dunning, among others, takes it for granted
that sport has an important social role, and tries to explain
it.[3] Their work has moved the study of sport, if not into
the mainstream of sociological work, then into a flowing
tributary: the sociology of sport has joined the social and
economic history of sport as an academic growth area in
the last fifteen years, and many courses in the sociology of
sport are offered at degree level.

In literary studies and criticism, on the other hand, the

situation is arguably still one of uncomprehending rejection. For all the bravery of T.S. Eliot, who included the FA Cup Final in the list of English cultural practices in his influential essay 'Notes towards the Definition of Culture' of 1948, the barriers of the concept of 'high culture', which kept certain types of literature, music and art at arm's length, had no difficulty in excluding physical recreation altogether. This means among other things that there is no developed sense of sporting aesthetics; no sense of exactly what it is in sporting activity that gives either the participant, or the observer, so much pleasure; and no sense of the continuous importance of writing about sport as a part of 'literature'. It is no answer to this problem to say that there are no aesthetic absolutes, or that the whole concept of aesthetics is philosophically dubious, and that therefore it does not matter that sport is excluded. If popular culture really is important, if one third of the world's population is prepared to watch certain sporting events on television (the only rival to this global popularity is certain types of music), we need to ask what pleasures they gain from this form of consumption – and we need to provide an answer, however contingent.

Cultural studies has not ignored sport altogether, where it is a component of other fields of study. In the investigation of the media, or the cultural construction of gender, sport may become an object of study in its turn – there have been illuminating studies of sport on television, as there have of television soaps or television news;[4] there have been useful studies of sport and the construction of both masculinity and femininity, as there have of the masculine and feminine images in advertising, say.[5] But sport in itself scarcely ever receives the limelight: it is hardly ever the starting point for an investigation. The 1993 Media, Communications and Cultural Studies catalogue from publishers Routledge listed 274 books. Only two of these dealt with sport – one was devoted to the relationship between sport and television, the other a cultural geography of soccer, space and landscape. Another aspect of leisure studies, the phenomenon of 'heritage culture', by contrast, had a section of this catalogue to itself with eighteen entries. A 1993 Routledge 'text book', the massive *Cultural Studies Reader*, has one entry (of twenty-eight) which deals directly with sport.[6] The absence is not confined to book publishing. The leading British cultural studies journal *New Formations*, after its first eight years of comment on contemporary theoretical debates and social practices, had published no articles at all on sport; the American journal *Cultural Studies*, also in its first eight years, had published precisely four (one of which merely took a sporting contest, the America's Cup yacht race, as the starting point for an analysis of urban photography). The British bimonthly magazine *The Modern Review*, which for four years in the early 1990s proudly proclaimed its mission to provide commentary on 'low culture for highbrows' was in some ways rather less depressing – many of its contributors referred casually to sporting personalities and events as points of comparison, in the expectation that the reader would be able to decode such references immediately; one of its constant literary points of reference was the amusing autobiography by soccer fan Nick Hornby, *Fever Pitch*. Even here, however, there were only six articles on sport in the review's first eleven issues (four on football, one each on tennis and boxing).

To continue along the deconstructive path for a moment, it should be emphasised that the absence is most glaring in books and articles which deal with aspects of the contemporary world which are unimaginable without sport. Take three books published in the early 1990s and devoted respectively to the body in postmodern theory, to debates about masculinity, and to contemporary youth culture – in all of which, arguably, the consideration of sport could play an important role. *The Body: Social Process and Social Theory* has one article of sixteen, a discussion of the 'martial art' aikido; one other article in this collection (on consumer culture) briefly discusses keep-fit sports such as jogging and aerobics.[7] *Unwrapping Masculinity* mentions sport once, tangentially, in an article about white male fears of black male sexuality.[8] *Common Culture*, a study of the ability of young people to interpret their own lives, includes only one connected sequence on sport, a seven-page discussion of sporting practices by young men and women which begins promisingly, discussing a wide range of activities (including swimming, walking, darts, snooker and yoga), but quickly tails off into a discussion of the beliefs and practices of male soccer fans.[9]

Soccer, and especially crowd behaviour at soccer matches, provides the only recurrent reference point to the sporting world from within cultural studies. There are simple historical reasons for this. Cultural Studies as a body of writing emerged in Britain in the 1960s. One of its subjects of study, shared with work in sociology, was male working-class youth; one of the objects of desire shared among male working-class youth was soccer, and one of the ways in which this affiliation was expressed was the growing phenomenon of 'football hooliganism'. For academics on the left, soccer therefore provided the opportunity to study an aspect of male working-class youth culture which, because it crudely opposed youth to authority, they thought of as oppositional and subversive. Sociologists came up with a reasoned explanation for this behaviour. The soccer authorities, it was claimed, were trying to deliver what had been a working-class game to a new middle-class audience; football hooliganism resisted this process.[10] There was more to it than symbolic class struggle, however. The continuing growth of the phenomenon of football hooliganism, and its alliance with racism and other aspects of extreme right-wing politics through the 1970s and 1980s, then allowed academics to do what they like best, contesting the theories of previous generations of academic writers; and the crowd in professional soccer has continued to be the one area of sport in which there has been consistent interest from cultural studies as well as sociology.[11] Work in the history of sport has also tended to privilege soccer.[12]

Even in the case of the British analysis of soccer and its crowds, however, we notice the absences: while there is some encouraging recent work, by and large work on 'the crowd' is actually about young men; there has been very little study of the older soccer fan, or the female spectator; or (perhaps surprisingly) of the players, or (less surprisingly?) of the officials, or management hierarchies; there has been very little study of the journalism of the game.[13] All these areas could and should provide information for any student of contemporary culture.

Investigative work could and should be done on – for
example – the class, ethnic and gender identities of sports
observers and participants in soccer, or other urban and
rural sports. Cultural studies could also profitably
investigate the availability and use of public and private
facilities, in order to comment on the relationship of sports
equipment, performance and personal identity. And all
these areas of sport in general could and should illuminate
the theoretical and empirical studies which pour from the
presses under the cultural studies rubric, many of them
under the subheading 'popular culture'.

What cultural studies has done most usefully with other
aspects of popular culture has been to question them
deconstructively, to reveal and comment on their role in
the construction of 'common sense'. One of the crucial
arguments in this book will be that particular kinds of
common sense, including versions of patriotism and
nationalism, and particular forms of personal identity
(some of which undercut those versions of patriotism and
nationalism), are available more powerfully and effectively
through aspects of sport – its performance and
technology, language and representation – than through
any other set of human activities and beliefs. Again, this
should serve to underline the importance of sport as a
field of study. If sport remains on the margin of cultural
studies or sociology, then it will be, as it so often is,
naturalised: in other words, it will be seen as simply natural
that people indulge in sporting activity, and the personal,
social and political consequences from that activity will
continue. We must examine the assumption that any
activity is 'natural'. Two examples. 'All kids kick balls in the
park, don't they?' Well, maybe most boys do – what about
girls? If girls don't play football, why not? Do we want to
naturalise competitive sport as an aspect of masculinity,
and passivity and uncompetitiveness as aspects of
femininity? Or: 'Everyone in the office is on the squash
ladder'. What happens if you don't want to or can't play
squash? Do you resign? Will you lose any chance of
promotion? Why are competitive games so important to
local (educational or workplace) let alone regional or
national politics? Why doesn't cultural studies want to ask,
let alone to answer these questions?

Perhaps the theoretical positions adopted by cultural studies work simply can't cope with sport. One assumption might be that cultural studies is heavily based on the interpretation of texts and other systems of linguistic interaction. The critical approaches used in most cultural studies work, which are derived from structuralism and poststructuralism and associated work in psychoanalysis, tend to see the explicable world as a series of interlocking sets of language-based symbols or 'discourses'.[14] Since sport is a physical activity, there is at least the problem of its language: how to describe non-linguistic communicative activity adequately; how to read the physical interactions of sport as a sign-system, how to *translate* those signs. Other physical entities and activities pose similar problems. Dance, and the *sound* of music, are also areas of experience which cultural studies has either neglected and/or failed to theorise adequately – though in the case of music, exciting work is currently under way to rectify the omission.[15]

One position common to many theoretical positions derived from structuralism and poststructuralism would be to avoid the problem by denying that there is any reality to which we can have access, apart from discourse itself. In other words we can only talk, and only understand the world, through words, whose meanings rely on their relations with each other, not to something real, 'out there' beyond language. This is a perfect recipe for scholarly activity (words about words) and political quietism; there is not enough space here to provide an elegant refutation of this theoretical position, but enough to say that it is not a position I find convincing. The assumption in this book is that people use words to describe and account for things which really exist, and that meaning occurs when people agree on the relationship between the verbal and the non-verbal, not on the differences between words.

Even for the fully paid-up poststructuralist, however, there's still no excuse for the comparative absence of sport from the cultural studies curriculum. Sport is about the body; it is not of itself merely textual – but it *generates text* by the yard: there is a whole world of sporting discourse waiting to be analysed. As well as the generous coverage in newspapers, there are dedicated magazines, and books:

biographies and autobiographies of players, books about teams and managers, books detailing how to play or to improve performance, histories of particular sports, and books of sporting records and statistics. Every summer a 1300 page book, a statistical compilation with a few introductory essays, *Wisden Cricketer's Almanack*, enters the British bestseller lists for two months or more. (An equivalent and equally massive compilation, *Cricket in India*, sells well at the beginning of the Indian season). Behind the large number of texts like these, which are usually produced by general publishers, there are fanzines, magazines written by dedicated followers of particular sports and teams. Behind that level of writing there are massive numbers of conversations about sport, which take place in public and private, in the workplace and in leisure environments like pubs and bars. There are also reams of academic text; as well as the small but growing number of texts on the historical and sociological analyses of sport as culture, there is a great deal about sport as immediate process. 'Sports science' deals with the relationships between the biology and physics of the body, and the mechanics of its supporting technologies, and sports performance.[16] 'Sports psychology' analyses the mental processes needed for successful sports performance.[17] There is, in other words, plenty of text here bearing on this enormous chunk of popular culture, for the ardent poststructuralist to bite into. To be fair, there have been one or two interesting nibbles, as for example essays in Roland Barthes's influential *Mythologies*, in which he writes compellingly about the drama and tragedy of wrestling, which he sees as a battle between good and evil, and about the Tour de France cycle race, which he compares to a Greek epic voyage.[18] Two essays by Umberto Eco show how casual sports chatter can be seen through the poststructuralist perspective.[19]

Pierre Bourdieu, a theoretical sociologist, has used sport extensively in his work on the structure of contemporary societies; his examination of the ways in which status is achieved and maintained through 'cultures of difference' is a valuable way into a sociology of modern sport, and a clear reminder that there is more to sport than text.[20] Bourdieu suggests that social distinctions (by which he means both distinctions of class, and distinctions *within* classes) have different components. In talking of taste and knowledge, he uses the term 'cultural capital'; in talking of the body, he discusses its *habitus*. The body is used (walks, carries itself) differently by different social groups, and sport is one of the most important ways through which the body's 'habitus' is learned. For example, Bourdieu argues that middle-class people (and working-class women) in the gymnasium will train for fitness, suppleness; working-class men will work for muscular strength, an immediately visible sign of labouring masculinity. The language of the body is an important aspect of the language of class, taste, and social distinction.

In the context of the continuing absence of sport from within cultural studies, this book will address the language of sport: the body language. In the end, the argument will be that sport is important because it complements some of the most cherished assumptions of cultural theory: through the analysis of sport we can profitably work on questions of identity, pleasure and desire, and the body; in ways which cannot be approached in other work. No account of culture which continually collapses our experience back into spoken or written language, or which attempts to read systems of bodily signs as if they were the exact equivalent of a spoken or written language, can encompass the meaning of sport for the bodies which participate in sport, or observe that participation through whatever medium. As chapters four to six will argue, sport exceeds linguistic signification, and certainly cannot be reduced to it.

This is principally because sport is first and foremost of the body, and important though it is as a component of journalistic, medical, scientific and commercial discourses, it is through the working of the body that sport operates. This does not mean that 'the body' is some kind of fixed entity operating outside time, space and cultural constraint – though this is just the kind of assumption often made in sports science, and even in histories of sport. There is no grand narrative of bodily changes which can encompass the body's relationship to sport. The common biographical narrative of growth and decay highlighting events such as birth, puberty, menarche, prime, menopause, aging and death are interrupted in the body of the sports performer by developments such as unusual muscular growth, or severe injury, or the use of corrective surgery or drugs, any or all of which may delay or hasten the onset of puberty, or aging, or even cause premature death. And in almost all sport the body of the performer is constrained by the rules of the competition, which may restrict the positioning of the arms and legs, the ability to lift feet from the ground, and so on: the culture of sport controls and directs bodily movement, as well as the shape of the body. (Where this control is seen to fail, the sport itself will fail. That most sublime essay in buttock-pumping, road walking, is commonly agreed to be a farce; virtually all the competitors break the fundamental rule of the contest, that one foot must be in contact with the ground at all times. Athletics reporters and commentators can see this, and don't take it seriously, so road walking is seldom reported, and may soon cease to be a competitive event.)

So in order to illuminate the relationships through which the sporting body operates, this book will discuss sport as a historical, geographical, technological, and cultural phenomenon. This will necessarily mean interrogating sport in relation to some of the key words of cultural studies and its associated disciplines: attention will be paid to questions of capital and commerce, science and technology, state and power, nation and empire, nature and authenticity, class, gender, ethnicity and sexuality. Sport will be seen in relation to debates about psychoanalytic, postcolonial, poststructuralist and postmodernist theory. By the end of the book, it is to be hoped, the reader will agree that the comparative absence of sport as a category within cultural studies is regrettable.

Narrative: Structuring Time and Place

Cultural studies draws from a common concern of both literary theory and history, a concern about *narration* – the telling of stories, and the ways in which they are told. People's senses of memory and identity depend on a sense of time and place which is usually organised through narratives, of among other things their lives and careers, the birth and progress of their children, the lives and deaths of their parents, and their own movements towards death. Sometimes these narratives are organised formally and personally, through diaries, autobiographies and other writings. For most people, however, they are structured through other systems, through personal forms such as letters, photographs, and other mementos, or through shared forms such as television, radio, and newspapers, and cultural products like music and dance. In all these sport can help to organise the narrative of place, time and identity. The memories of participation or spectatorship; the certificates and trophies of the youthful athlete, proudly displayed in the middle-aged lawyer's study; the cards from a lifetime's attendance at race meetings; songs and movements associated with victories or defeats; all can place people in their own time and space. As the anthropologist Clifford Geertz put it in an influential essay on cock-fighting in Bali, sport is 'deep play', thoroughly worked into our ways of seeing the world, 'a story we tell ourselves about ourselves'.[21] Its story organises our lives, our histories.

One of the crucial roles played by sport is that of delineating and confirming a sense of place. From the stadia of the inner city, the ballparks and soccer grounds, through the suburban tennis clubs and city-edge race tracks, to the massive shooting estates of the very wealthy, the various types of building or other geographical structures which contain the sporting contest reaffirm physical, geographical boundaries. Sports like orienteering, rally driving and the cycling tour explore regions and nations as geographical entities, offering knowledge of those places to the participants and also to the television observers of the events. The Paris-Dakar rally celebrates the former French Empire. The Monte Carlo rally, in which competing cars start from different places within Europe, is a celebration of European unity. The most obvious, but perhaps still the most important of these events is the cycling Tour de France, which still involves the whole French community in a national celebration of the existence of France as a topographical entity. The many different landscapes are combined with the people who move on their surface (city dwellers and rural communities from the chosen route are the focus of pre-race publicity; some towns actually pay to be included on the route), and both are reconfirmed as part of the nation through the narrative of the race itself.

Or, one should perhaps say, *were* reconfirmed; this unity is not unproblematic. Two outstanding Tour champions of recent years have been the American Greg LeMond and the Belgian Eddie Merckx. Even geographically, the Tour was never a simple monument to place and nation (it started as a newspaper promotion); the growing idea of the unity of Europe, the commercial imperatives of sponsors, and television companies seeking wider audiences, have together fractured this unity in recent years.[22] The tour has often crossed into Belgium, and the decision to take the 1994 race over the English Channel into Kent, Sussex and Hampshire for a few days pedalling around the Weald and North and South Downs has undoubtedly fractured the 'Frenchness' of the race (though there is topographically at least an argument for including the chalk landscape of the South Downs, which is continuous with that of Normandy, while historically the two nations were once politically united).

Sport, therefore, can offer a narrative of both an individual and a collective identity; but like most narratives, it can be disruptive as well as confirmatory. Towns, regions and nations will constantly reflect on the sports currently played, the players and successes of the past, and will plan for sporting activities and achievements in the future. Again these reflections and aspirations are often formally structured, in written histories, in museums and exhibitions, or in the building of facilities like racetracks or swimming pools, which are often deliberately constructed as 'the national stadium', or 'to Olympic standard'. Though they may aim to symbolise the pride of particular areas, such buildings can often be at the expense of local communities whose houses are demolished to make way for sports facilities, as was the case in Manchester, England in the early 1990s as that city sought (unsuccessfully) the privilege and profit of hosting the Olympic Games in the year 2000. Less formally, and less disruptively, reflection and aspiration take place through fans' publications and meetings of supporters' associations and sports clubs, or just the shared memories and fantasies of chatter at a social club. By sharing these memories people can place themselves as part of a larger narrative of place and time.

Routinely, the sporting calendar is a constant reminder of the way in which time is a structured part of ideas of national culture. Nations and other communities are imagined, in part, within the passing of the seasons and years. The English sporting year, for instance, with its list of events of national importance, constantly renarrates, reorganises time. From the rugby union internationals at the start of the year, the Grand National at the start of spring, the soccer FA Cup final and the Derby at the start of summer, the Wimbledon tennis championships and the Test matches in high summer, to the first Saturday of the soccer season at the onset of autumn, these points in the calendar stand as reminders of an achieved constancy, and of the grand organising meta-narrative of all this, 'Englishness'. But they also, simultaneously, signify that the players within that story – by implication, all the English – are constantly changing: the rise to dominance of working-class soccer players at the end of the nineteenth century, or the increasing presence of successful black players in athletics, rugby, soccer and cricket teams representing England, and the gradual increase in media exposure given to women's sporting competitions in golf, soccer and cricket, underline the point that this *is* a narrative, a developing story, and not simply a calendar subject to constant repetition. A similar story can be told of any other country, or region. Particular versions of the repeated events are immediately absorbed into the meta-narrative, becoming part of the national memory, often through association with particular individual stories. Again to take the English example, Stanley Matthews's Cup Final in 1953, Virginia Wade's Wimbledon in 1976, Red Rum's four triumphs in the Grand National in the early 1980s, and Linford Christie's victory in the 100 metres at Barcelona in the 1992 Olympics, have all attained the status of national myth: not least because in each case the per- former was him or herself defying time and reaching success late in their careers.

Structuring Thought: Ideology

This emphasis on the manufacture of memory, and on myth, has been an important contribution made by cultural studies to the reworking of history as *cultural* history. There is a related approach in which cultural studies views questions of memory and identity through the terms of psychoanalysis. The fine details of this mode of investigation, and even its main assumptions, remain controversial, but the study of film and literature would be very different today without the insights offered by psychoanalytic theory, and cultural studies has borrowed from these approaches in its considerations of popular culture, which can easily be applied to sport. Three aspects are important here. Firstly, memory is not all-inclusive: not everything that happens is kept in the memory. Secondly, much of what is not kept in the forefront of memory recedes into the subconscious or unconscious mind, from which it may or may not refract back into consciousness. The mind has a multilayered life of its own, in other words – not all of it is immediately subject to control or even to rational analysis. Thirdly, partly because of this, *fantasy* and *desire* are crucial identity formants. Sport is clearly, for anyone remotely interested in it, the subject of fantasy and desire. Participants and spectators alike desire success and fantasise about achieving it. One popular form of gambling is 'fantasy football', in which members of the public choose their own teams from among those playing the professional sport, a computer allocates points to the fantasy teams based on the actual players' performance, and the winner is the person whose fantasy 'team' wins the championship at the end of the season. Fantasy is a crucial, and active, part of the sporting world. Without these drives, competitive sport would be impossible. Their presence, however, suggests very strongly that the narratives of personal and collective memory are also subject to fantasy and desire: the narratives of history, whether individual or national, partake of myth. Sportspeople are worshipped as heroines/heroes and denigrated as villains, I suggest, because of the power of our individual desires.

One concept which remains useful in its attempt to

apply the insights of psychoanalysis to the wider structures of society is the concept of 'ideology'. This is a much-abused term, but there is nothing necessarily difficult about it. My use is rather different from that blanket concept of the 'dominant ideology' which was mentioned above in relation to the Yeos' paranoid view of sporting culture. What I mean here by ideology is a set of rules about the way society works which are not written down and learned formally, but which people learn and practise through informal contact and which operate largely unconsciously, as common sense. Individuals are addressed as members of society through this ideology – it instructs them, again unconsciously, 'hailing them into position' as useful citizens.

It is important to avoid conspiracy theory here. Some people still insist that ideologies belong to classes, and that the dominant ideology within any given society is the one which includes the values of that society and which helps to reproduce it, always in the interests of the dominant class. As a sociological model for the analysis of systems of beliefs and values, this may be useful. Otherwise it has very little to recommend it, because it has no room for any kind of change. If we all learnt a single, monolithic dominant ideology along with language, one political and economic system would remain dominant for ever. If, however, we think of different aspects of the workings of society as carrying their own ideologies – aspects such as religion, business, education and government – the term becomes more fruitful. Ideologies inform aspects of people's lives, but do not dictate the whole of them.[23] The beliefs of the social historians the Yeos have already been referred to as an ideology – in this case they were writing within a professional, educational ideology whose goal was the transformation of society to socialism. Their rather naively optimistic political agenda presumably did not prevent those authors from considering some of their experiences to be pleasurable, whatever their written beliefs. This book will take it for granted that people are addressed by different, sometimes contradictory, ideologies. It is difficult, for example, to be both a pro-abortion liberal and a Roman Catholic: both have different ideologies about what it is to be human, and the rights and obligations pertaining to humanity; individual identities are fractured by this contradiction. Similarly, within sport, it is difficult to be both a freelance professional (where the priority is to earn money) and to be an international performer (where the priority is to represent the nation); it is difficult to be either and to believe in the ideology of fair play (where the priority is to compete without unfair advantage on either side; without 'cheating'): the identities of many top sportspeople are equally fractured by these contradictions.

Ideologies, in this sense, are a complementary part of the narratives through which people construct the meanings of their lives. Through their fantasies, desires and ideological beliefs they will interpret the basic data of the sporting world – changes in their own golf handicaps, or their children's progress as tennis players, as much as the progress of 'their' local or national professional baseball or hockey teams. The same events – say, personal successes like a good golf round, or a local badminton tournament won, or collectively, a national victory on the football field, or defeats in the same contests – will be differently interpreted according to fantasies of success, and broader ideologies of personal performance, childhood, and nationality; through this matrix of ideologies, beliefs and desires the narrative of personal, familial or national growth to success (or decline through failure) will be constructed.

Structuring Thought: Fantasy and Desire

I suggest, then, that ideologies are a complementary part of these narratives of everyday life. But I do not want to reduce everything that is thought, said or felt to the status of ideology. People are driven not just by agreed collective explanations of the world but also by their personal relationship with those explanations; personal experience contains memories, fantasies and desires which are not simply ideological. These aspects of experience and thought are difficult to separate (one might ask, for example, at what point does an event enter memory? At what point if any can we say that a desire has been achieved? Do we experience an event immediately, without the screen of ideology, and then interpret it, or are we always interpreting what we see, hear and feel?); but for analytical purposes it is useful to distinguish between memory and fantasy. Memory I will here delineate as a sense of the personal and collective past. Fantasy is a more complex term, which involves the relationship between memory, the experience of the present, and the imagining of the future. It is a reflexive and indirect way of mediating our relationship to the world, informed by a sense of the inadequacies and possibilities of both the past and the present, including the ideologies associated with 'common sense', of personal position, which help to define our senses of the inadequate and the possible. By working through those elements, fantasy's desires help to produce our ideas about the future – and therefore they help to produce the future itself. Desires can, of course, be sexual or political, and though they are experienced by the individual, they often concern the familial or collective future. In the analysis offered in this book, memory is about the past, ideology about the present, and fantasy a way of seeing beyond the present and desiring the future. But of course all these forces interact constantly to produce the overall realisation of the world, the stories we tell ourselves of ourselves: the narratives of everyday life.

Well, yes, my patient reader will no doubt remark at this point, but what if anything has this to do with sport? Sport, that reader continues, isn't a narrative of everyday life – it is about the extraordinary, the privileged moments of our lives whether as participants or spectators. It concerns the heroic pursuit of championships or physically improbable records by people who are athletically gifted above the average, and the wholehearted identification with them in these moments by spectators, commentators and so on.

There are two answers to this objection; both are important. Firstly, sport exists at the personal level. It is an increasingly important way in which people relate to their own bodies, through the personal regime of healthy diet and regular exercise, often directed by professional teachers in classes such as aerobics, or circuit training in gymnasiums; or in more directly personal forms of exercise such as hill walking or jogging. These forms of

sport are clearly ideological, and involve our own desires
and fantasies: they construct us as subjects of the perfect,
ideal body we wish to own and inhabit; through these
desires they construct us as consumers, as we buy the
services of professional trainers, and as we buy gear such
as training shoes and walking boots. Aerobics, for instance,
is a form of collective, comparative policing of the body,
which tries to establish a common shape (in relation to
common ideas about sexuality and sexual attractiveness,
age, ethnic and gender position); jogging is a self-policing
exercise directed to the same end.

Secondly, even the professional sports beloved of the
media are part of the same process. They provide many of
the ideal bodies to which the rest of us aspire. In many
cases these also model the clothes which we sports-placed
consumers can buy as we seek to realise these desires (in
women this general effect is often enhanced by a very
deliberate and very lucrative glamorisation, as for example
with American sprinter Florence Joyner-Griffith, who
always ran in eye-catching, sponsored outfits, or the
American tennis player Jennifer Capriati, who was once
paid $600,000 to model a haircut on court). High
achievers in sport become role models/clothes models in
this way. These narratives of sporting achievement,
therefore, are also, always, part of the narratives of
personal position, class and gender, race and ethnicity,
and nation. All these, always, are part of sport. As this
book will demonstrate, sport in its contemporary presence
would be impossible, quite literally unthinkable, without
them, and we can only understand sport in relation to
these aspects of our consciousness, our past and the
desires we have of the future. Sport is part of everyday
discourse, and its language is that of everyday life,
constructing and reconstructing the identities of participants and observers alike.

Headlines in Context

To underline these very general statements, I shall
mention two examples of the ways in which these wider
social and personal meanings are present in the discourses

of sport. Two rather different banners, in fact, through which we can read the ways in which sport is continually part of, interpreted through, and made by histories, ideologies and fantasies.

In the summer of 1984, the English cricket season was centred around a tour by the strongest side in the world, West Indies. The visitors proved their strength by defeating the side representing England in all five of the Test matches: an unparalleled achievement for them, and a catastrophic defeat for England (though not the last: West Indies then repeated the dose. After first defeating Australia six times in Australia, they then gave England a further five-nil thrashing in the Caribbean). It was a particularly joyful occasion for the players representing the combined West Indian islands, and their supporters in England. At the end of the final Test of the series, as the crowd gathered in front of the pavilion of the Oval cricket ground, a West Indian supporter proudly unfurled a banner containing the single, striking pun BLACKWASH. The banner was a powerful symbol of the continuing relationship between Britain and this group of former colonies: the success of the West Indian team, and the game of cricket, in drawing together and representing the very different communities in the West Indies, offset against the continuing postcolonial legacy of racism, directed at the West Indian community in Britain; and the impossible basis of that racism, the belief that black people are somehow inferior to whites. The five-win Blackwash and its banner symbol seemed to proclaim a very different superiority.

In his book *Beyond a Boundary*, the Trinidadian marxist historian C.L.R. James explores the place of cricket in the unfolding history of imperial Britain and the Caribbean.[24] He examines the importance of the game to an area which the legacy of genocide, slavery and the continuing domination of British capital, administration, education and culture had effectively denied a history. James insists that triumph at cricket, especially victory over the former coloniser, is crucial to the Caribbean sense of self-worth. It makes that history. Every great achievement by a West Indian at Lord's, the West London ground considered to be the headquarters of world cricket (such as the astonishing double century with which batsman Gordon Greenidge won the Lord's Test of that summer of 1984) is an affirmative political act, and a sign of maturity, independence and equality. The five-Test Blackwash implied that cultural superiority had been achieved. Memory, fantasy and desire had combined to produce a team whose victory had combatted the fantasy of racism, and which may have helped to produce more positive images of black people in Britain. Though it could also have increased the white fear of black people, especially of the black male body which is one of the fantasy-bases of white racism, there was no escaping the sporting achievement. The host country, the former imperial power and the inventor of cricket, had been beaten at its own game by those to whom in some ways it denied equal opportunity.

Cricket is now, it seems, in decline in the West Indies. This is often attributed to the influence of global American culture; beamed across the Caribbean by American television, basketball and baseball are seen as ways in which young West Indians can improve their lives. While this may be true enough, I would also suggest that the crushing of English cricket since the 1970s, culminating in the two Blackwashes, has in some way released a psychic tie. Having achieved total domination, there was nowhere else for West Indian cricket to go.

The second banner is a newspaper headline. After Sally Gunnell had won the 200 metre hurdles at the 1992 Olympic Games in Barcelona, she appeared on the victory rostrum draped in the Union Flag. The following day, next to a front page photograph of this occasion, The *Sun* newspaper displayed the banner headline IT'S TRUE: ESSEX GIRLS DO COME FIRST. Here, behind the apparently joyous celebration of a triumph by a popular national representative, there is a regressive fantasy at work, one which constructs a deeply conservative ideology of gender relations.

The *Sun*'s headline is a signal of an important moment in the politics of class and gender in Britain. During the 1980s, as the upwardly mobile flocked to the banner of Thatcherism, 'Essex Man' was identified as a particular type of the new conservatism. Young, and comparatively wealthy (whether a worker in the aggressively expanding financial centre of the City of London or a self-employed plumber), Essex Man became the butt of a particularly condescending humour – a rather different type of conservatism. He lacked the cultural capital of a high-value education, and his alleged dress sense (white socks), and taste in cars (fast Fords), drink (lager) and home decoration (Artexed ceilings inside, stone cladding outside) were assailed vigorously by the 'quality' press, and through the wit of middle-class comedians – for example, Harry Enfield's creation 'Loadsamoney'. A genre of humour, the Essex Man joke, was born. This was all resentful snobbery, aimed at somehow putting these upstarts back in their places in the discursive order (if not the economic order, a function which was fulfilled more than adequately by the recession of the early 1990s).

The Essex Man joke had an equivalent, the 'Essex Girl' joke, which was unsubtly different, as the loaded term 'girl' implies. Where Essex Man jokes were about low cultural capital allied with the ostentatious display of money and the freedom it affords, Essex Girl jokes were all about the free exercise of female sexuality (e.g. 'How does Essex Girl put the light on after sex? She kicks the car door open'). Again, these jokes were intended to put women in their place, to restrict the freedom of young women to be single and sexually active; to reassert the 'values' of the family, which is still in some quarters the only institution in which female sexual activity is welcome.

So even at the moment of national triumph for an athlete at the Olympic games, the most prestigious athletic meeting of all, that particularly reactionary newspaper, the *Sun*, saw fit to display its anti-woman politics. A reactionary male fantasy, which can both enjoy, desire and fantasise about the idea of an open female sexuality (not least in the *Sun*, whose pages since the 1970s have included the display of topless models) and feel deeply threatened by it, worked on a sporting event to proclaim a conservative politics of gender. As we shall see, women participating in sport have often been faced with ideological battles of this kind.

Nevertheless, the very fact that I have produced this kind of reading should indicate that there is no simple relationship between the political intent of a message and its interpretation. Our understandings are not simply produced by messages given to us: we actively interpret them, through a grid formed by our own unique experiences of the world – which is precisely why we need to differentiate analytically between external message-bearing ideology, and internal memory, fantasy, and desire. The language which surrounds sport surrounds most people; it is itself part of the grid, constantly supplying metaphors for other activities. But there is more to sport than language, however headlines are written. The body of the athlete, which is the site of public desire and fear in the case of both Sally Gunnell and West Indian cricketers, is not reducible to any single message, or even a set of messages: the body is more than mere language. This is one of the reasons for its power – and one reason for the influence and importance of sport. Memory, fantasy and desire play upon the body as it matures and changes shape, and as its potential changes and develops: sport plays an important part in this process, helping to link the work of body and mind.

The Imagined Community

An old-fashioned sociology, or social history, of sport might happily talk about relations of class, gender and ethnicity within sports and wider society. It might talk about technological change, about relations between capital and labour, spectator, player and owner, about the place of women in sport, the rise of corporate sponsorship of teams or events, or the increasing 'abuse' of drugs in the pursuit of sporting success. All these aspects of sport will be present here, but the book will continuously reflect on the relationships between fantasy and memory, ideology and narrative in contemporary sport. Again, as the examples of Gunnell and the West Indian cricketers show, one illuminating aspect of these relationships is the role sport can play in the creation of a sense of nation, an 'imagined community' in Benedict Anderson's phrase.

Anderson's useful book, *Imagined Communities*, sees the community as necessarily a product of the imagination.[25]

Where we cannot know everyone, we have to have a mental picture of the world in which we live, and especially of the people we identify with as members of the same region or nation. The family, formal education and the media play important roles in this process, constantly addressing us as citizens, neighbours, kin and so on. Through this address, this ideologically driven set of narratives, we build our imagined communities. Anderson is concerned in particular with the nation, which we imagine, he claims, as inherently *limited* by geographical boundaries, and *sovereign* (able to exist freely and independently, passing and administering its own laws). Sport is clearly an important way in and through which the nation is narrated. Virtually all sports are contested and reported at the level of international competition; international sporting success is usually reported in the winning country as national triumph, thus reinforcing the sense of 'horizontal comradeship' Anderson believes to be so important in the making of communities for which people gladly kill – and die. Sport is not, unfortunately, a category given much attention by Anderson. The analysis offered by this book sees sport as an important part of the modern state, based around the often highly artificial distinctions of 'nation': sporting contests have formed an important part of the imagined community of the nation since the end of the nineteenth century.

In the post-war, and especially the post-Cold War world, these distinctions are, however, coming to seem increasingly artificial. In an age of instant global communication, and swift transcontinental travel, there is less necessary identification with that particular form of imagined community, the modern nation state. Personal and collective affiliations deriving from language, culture, place of origin and religion are at least as important. To some commentators, indeed, the nation is anachronistic precisely because it is 'modern', associated in other words with the 'modernity' which emerged in late nineteenth century Europe. This is a distinct historical period which some would say ended in 1945, or at latest with the collapse of the Russian empire at the end of the 1980s. Since the break-up of the European empires and/or the end of the Cold War, the argument goes, we have entered both a 'postcolonial' and a 'postmodern' age. Along with this (and perhaps because of it), the stability of personal identities, which was always fragile, has been further thrown into question. The human subjects of postmodernity are fractured internally as much as externally, without the comfort of collective grand narratives to hold onto. Class has lost its primacy in the 'grand narrative' of social construction; sexualities, gender roles, and ethnic identities are less certain, and identities and choices based around the personal and the body are more important. The question arises, therefore: is the imagined community of the nation more, or less, important in the condition of postmodernity – and if so, what communities do we imagine? If sport was important to the nation, is it as important to the imagining of the new worlds we inhabit?

Imagining Sport

The book attempts to offer a way in which key insights about desire, narration and identity can illuminate our understanding of sport. In the second and third chapters I begin to identify the processes through which sport is played, and through which sport plays a part in contemporary society, by examining the relationship between sport and nation: aspects of the language of sport, and some of the theories used to analyse it, will be identified. Some of the issues first raised here will be explored in detail in the rest of the book, in chapters on collective and individual identities, power and technology, and sporting discourse. Finally, the argument will turn to the pleasures of sport. By this time, hopefully, the importance of sport to cultural studies will be obvious.

One first issue, which must be addressed before the analysis can proceed, is the deceptively simple question: what is sport? There is not space here to debate the issue fully, or even to decide what particular activities can be classed as sports. For the social historian Johan Huizinga, the distinctive mark of humanity is the propensity to ritualise activities, to make them into games: he referred to humanity as *homo ludens*, 'man' the games-player, and he insisted that sports and games were part of this continuum of ritualised activities. Clearly beyond this the definition differs in time and place, including the common distinction between sports and games. Activities like bridge, chess, and computer and video games, even board games like Monopoly, all are highly ritualised activities, regulated by rules of play. All are competitive (in the case of video games, competition can be against the self, against the previous best time, or against the clock, as well as against the machine's program, and/or a human opponent); all test the nerve and skill of their participants. Bridge and chess are also professionalised activities which can earn their participants large sums of money. It could be argued that these sedentary activities do not count as sport because they do not involve intense physical activity: that we must differentiate between competitive games in general, and sport, which has this physical element.

On the other hand, potholing or mountaineering would not be in everyone's list of sports, despite the intense, skillful, even dangerous physical activity involved, because they do not usually involve competition between individuals or groups of individuals. There are, in fact, many organised climbs which do involve competition in this sense, but more importantly in almost all cases there is internal competition, the test of the climber and appropriate equipment against her or his own willpower and musculature (as well as against the terrain and weather). Failure can mean death, as it did for Alison Hargreaves, who attempted to follow her successful climb of Everest in March 1995 with the more difficult ascent of K2 in the following August. Here it will be taken for granted that these physical activities are sports – defeat's opposite here, the victory, is success in the climb, rather than victory over a human opponent. Leisure sports such as aerobics, jogging and circuit training for personal fitness also involve this element of personal internal competition; here they will also be counted as sports.

Another difficulty is the place of the traditional field sports of hunting, shooting and fishing. Shooting and fishing may involve competition (against other hunters as well as the prey animal or other target), but the role of the performer is not always intensely physical, quite the reverse in some forms of fishing; fox, mink or deer hunting involve the vicarious physical competition between animals, with human competition of secondary importance. How far can they be seen as sports in the same sense as the post-industrial team games like hockey? For some writers they are relics of the pre-modern sporting age. They are arguably, however, as modern as any other sport, and as subject to the same pressures of commercialism, with the technologies of clothing, gun, or rod, line and fly design, under constant research and development. While they are seen as sports for the purposes of this book, these issues are further explored in the second chapter.

In order to further the argument and to enter that second chapter, I now propose a working definition of sport as one which accepts the notions of public competition involving physical activity. While, as the rest of the book will make clear, this definition is as undoubtedly a historical and cultural construct as any other, it remains useful at least as a starting point in understanding the meaning of sport in contemporary society:

> Sport is an activity involving the public practice of physical skills among individuals or teams, within agreed rules which are regulated by bureaucracies, and which control the permitted activities of the human or animal body, constraining the time and space permitted for the activity, and which award the laurel leaves of success to the individual or team achieving a required target.

This may sound familiar enough to anyone who has played or watched athletics, tennis, baseball or cricket, or organised a walking holiday – or even, at a pinch, played chess. But was it ever thus?

Notes

1. E. and S. Yeo (eds), *Popular Culture and Class Conflict*, Croom Helm, London 1981.

2. *See* T. Mason, *Association Football and English Society*, Harvester Press, Brighton 1980, and W. Vamplew, *The Turf: A Social and Economic History of Horse Racing*, Routledge, London 1976.

3. See for instance A. Guttmann, *From Ritual to Record*, Columbia University Press, New York 1978; Jennifer Hargreaves, *Sporting Females*, Routledge, London 1990; N. Elias and E. Dunning, *The Quest for Excitement: Sport and Leisure and the Civilising Process*, Blackwell, Oxford, 1986.

4. G. Whannel, *Fields in Vision: Television Sport and Cultural Transformation*, Routledge, London 1992.

5. Some recent examples are M. Messner and D. Sabo (eds), *Sport, Men and the Gender Order: Critical Feminist Perspectives*, Human Kinetics Press, Champaign, Illinois, 1990; B. Pronger, *The Arena of Masculinity: Sports, Homosexuality and the Meaning of Sex*, GMP Publishers, London, 1990; J. Hargreaves, *Sporting Females, op.cit.*

6. S. During (ed), *The Cultural Studies Reader* Routledge, London, 1993.

7. M. Featherstone, M. Hepworth and B.S. Turner (eds), *The Body: Social Process and Cultural Theory*, Sage, London 1991.

8. R. Chapman and J. Rutherford (eds), *Male Order: Unwrapping Masculinity*, Lawrence and Wishart, London 1990.

9. P. Willis, *Common Culture*, Open University Press, Milton Keynes, 1990.

10. The least worst of these apologias is R. Ingham *et al* (eds), *Football Hooliganism*, Inter-Action Imprint, London 1978.

11. S. Hall, 'The treatment of football hooliganism in the press', in *Football Hooliganism*, pp15-36; J. Williams *et al*, *Hooligans Abroad*, Routledge, London 1984; Second edition 1988.

12. For example, J. Walvin, *The People's Game*, Allen Lane, London 1975; T. Mason, *Association Football and English Society*, Harvester, Brighton 1980; but a general history like R. Holt, *Sport and the British*, (Oxford University Press, Oxford, 1989) also overconcentrates on soccer.

13. Closest to such an analysis is the work of Alex Fynn. See e.g. A. Fynn, L. Guest and P. Law, *The Secret Life of Football*, Macdonald/Queen Anne Press, 1989. For women soccer fans, see the forthcoming book by Anne Coddington, *Rough Girls*.

14. A very readable introduction to all this is R. Lapsley and M. Westlake, *Film Theory: An Introduction*, Manchester University Press, Manchester 1988.

15. For recent work on music see A. Moore, *Rock, the Primary Text*, Open University Press, Buckingham, 1993; S. Whiteley, *The Space. Between the Notes*, Routledge, London 1992; A. Blake, *The Land Without Music? The Sound of Twentieth Century Britain*, Manchester University Press, Manchester 1997.

16. See for example R. Hawkey, *Sports Science*, Hodder and Stoughton, London 1981; D.D. Arnhem, *Modern Principles of Athletic Training: The Science of Sports Medicine*, Times Mirror 1985; E.R. Burke, *Cycling, Health and Physiology: Using Sports Science to Improve Your Riding and Racing*, Vitesse Press, Battleboro, Vermont, 1992.

17. See e.g. R.N. Singer, *Coaching, Athletics and Psychology*, McGraw-Hill, London, 1971; R. Martens, *Coaches Guide to Sports Psychology*, Human Kinetics, Champaign, Illinois, 1987; G.C. Roberts, *Motivation in*

Sport and Exercise, Human Kinetics, Champaign, Illinois, 1992; and the less professional, more personal fitness advocacy in J. Douillard, *Body, Mind and Sport*, Bantam Books, London 1994.

18. R. Barthes, *Mythologies*, Paladin, London 1974.

19. U. Eco, *Travels in Hyperreality*, Pan, London 1987. My thanks to Richard Reynolds for this reference.

20. See P. Bourdieu, 'How Can One Be a Sports Fan?', essay of 1978 reprinted in During (ed), *op.cit.*, pp339-355; and in more general terms, P. Bourdieu, *Distinction: A Social Critique of the Judgement of Taste*, Routledge, London 1986.

21. C. Geertz, 'Cock-Fighting in Bali', quoted in R. Holt, *Sport and the British: A Modern History*, Oxford University Press, Oxford 1989.

22. See R. Holt, *Sport and Society in Modern France*, Macmillan, London 1981, Chapter 5, 'Cycling as a Commercial Spectacle'.

23. See the discussion in Chapter 2 of A. Blake, *Reading Victorian Fiction*, Macmillan, London 1989.

24. C.L.R. James, *Beyond A Boundary*, first edition Stanley Paul, London 1963; Serpent's Tail, London 1995.

25. B. Anderson, *Imagined Communities*, Verson, London 1984.

2   History, Modernity, Rationality

Sport is a characteristic of virtually all the past and present societies for which written or archaeological evidence survives. Wall paintings from Crete show young men and women vaulting over the backs of bulls. Reliefs sculpted into the walls at Chichen Itza, in Mexico, show a kind of football game, which is thought to be a ritual celebration by the Aztecs of the birth of the sun and moon; they also show the decapitation of one of the losing players. Historians and anthropologists have described many types of sporting contest in Africa, the most universal being various forms of wrestling; a hockey-like sport is illustrated in wall paintings from ancient Egypt. The origins of the equestrian hockey game, polo, have been traced to sixth-century Persia. In the steppes of Asia a polo-like game was and still is played – in this game the body of an animal is carried by opposing teams of horse riders towards a goal. There is one shared characteristic among all these precursors of contemporary sports. 'Ancient' sport was usually dangerous, often deliberately violent, and sometimes routinely involved the death of some of its human participants.

Greece and Rome

Sport was and is universal, part of all the human societies of which we have some record, but sport also has particular histories; one set of sporting activities and associated ideologies developed in western Europe and spread throughout the world – and it is this set of sports which are the main focus of this book. The sporting legacies of Greece and Rome are especially important for the ways in which this version of sport developed, although their impact has been greatest since the nineteenth century, when they helped to displace cultures of sporting activity which had grown in medieval and early modern Europe. These legacies are complex, and unravelling them will involve a long sidelong glance at theoretical models of sporting behaviour as well as histories of sports' development.

The cluster of mediterranean cultures known as the ancient Greeks held athletic meetings for religious purposes – the best known being the games held at Olympia in honour of the god Zeus: the Olympic Games.[1] Only male citizens were allowed to compete, and in many cases, including the Olympic Games, female citizens were not even allowed to watch; likewise the men and women who formed in most cases the majorities of these societies, the slaves and peasants, were not allowed to participate. (There was an equivalent women-only meeting dedicated to the goddess Hera, the Heratic Games).[2] The citizens worshipped their gods and goddesses in various forms of racing, wrestling and other combat sports, including the no-holds-barred fight called the Pankration. There were no team games, and no honours were available to those who finished second; in each contest a single winner was crowned. The successful athletes were held in high esteem in their communities, and were virtually full time professional performers. Greek sport, therefore, was *elitist*, excluding the lower classes, and rewarding only the strong and successful; it was *professional*, with successful participants making a living as athletes; and its participants were *representatives*, who competed for the honour of their cities as well as themselves.

Sport in Rome followed the professional path; perhaps the most important legacy here is the idea of *circus*, in which travelling entertainers take their competitions around the world. This is professional and elitist, but in the meritocratic sense, of participation and reward according to ability, rather than the social class which had been important to the Greek games. In many cases therefore there was an imperial star system, in which the notion of representation of place was less important – though there were chariot races in Rome itself whose teams attracted the same dedicated (and sometimes riotous) followings as today's urban team sports. Another legacy from Rome is the single combat between *gladiators*. The Roman idea of public entertainment included gladiatorial confrontations in which the loser was often killed; and there were also more directly murderous confrontations between professional killers and slaves, or the ritual killing of unarmed groups of criminals or heretics, including Christians. This slaughter was sometimes entrusted to animals (Christians really were fed to lions as a public spectacle); there were also confrontations between animals. Recent archaeological evidence has confirmed that these massacres for the entertainment of the public took place even in England, one of the farthest outposts of the empire; the circus travelled far.

Given this association of sport with pagan religion and with violence as public entertainment, it is hardly surprising that not all societies, or perhaps more accurately not all groups within societies, have welcomed the presence of sport. Fundamentalist Christian groups known as the Puritans, in seventeenth-century Britain and North America (like some Muslims in contemporary societies), turned their hostility into intervention, and tried to ban sporting activity, especially on holy days; the eventual failure of puritanism to control the pleasures of these days can be seen in the corruption of the words holy days into 'holidays', which are still associated with public participation in leisure practices including circuses and sports. And yet in the long term, it can be argued, the Puritan's intervention foreshadowed the creation of contemporary sport, which is very different from the sport which they tried to stop. As the types of contest we usually think of as sport, and their supporting ideals, which now occupy so much of global culture, first emerged in Britain, some reflections on the history of British sport, and on ways to interpret it, are in order. These will be followed by a trace through the history of international competition and consideration of some aspects of the contemporary sporting world.

Carnival or Puritanism – or Both?

To go back to that moment of Puritan intervention: what were they trying to ban? Sport in seventeenth-century Britain involved mass public participation as both participants and observers, in activities which were constrained by space and time. Behaviour, however, was often given license rather than controlled by rules. Sport was an aspect of carnival, in which normal rules of social hierarchy and acceptable behaviour were suspended or inverted. This is an important interpretative model. Our ideas about carnival owe much to the work of the Russian critic Bakhtin, who located his explorations of this phenomenon in the Europe of the early modern period (i.e. the sixteenth and seventeenth centuries), associating it with the writings of the French proto-novelist Rabelais.[3] The popular culture of the middle ages and the early modern period has been analysed in the work of many historians of Europe, especially France, who have interrogated various moments of puzzling popular excess such as the massacre of animals.[4] Through study of the legal and other records of such events they have pieced together a model of popular culture, and of the importance of carnival as a popular festival within it.

Bakhtin argued that carnival took place at specific times (say, Easter) and in specific spaces – usually the public spaces of the town or village, such as the village green or market square. In these locations, and for an agreed period, the normal flow of time was interrupted by what he called 'sacred time', during which the world was turned upside down. The normal hierarchy of power relations was inverted – for example people without power were crowned, while those with power became their servants. Bakhtin insisted that this reversal of power was paralleled by a difference in the prevailing modes of discourse. In normal times, the world was explained through a set of *monological* discourses. Monological explanations were unitary and closed, offering a single set of interpretations and incorporating the existing power structure. They were carried principally by the church and the law. In sacred time, however, the peoples' voices were heard, and monological discourses were replaced by *dialogical* interpretations of the world, which allowed for open-ended debate, interpretation and celebration. Aspects of these dialogic interpretations survive in popular song, and in the behaviour of the crowd at some sporting events; Bakhtin also pointed out that some subsequent types of literary text such as modernist poetry and fiction are also dialogical rather than the monological texts of the closed ending (e.g. final sentence 'She began to wonder about the next day's meeting. . .', as opposed to 'They all lived happilly ever after').

Here the world of cultural studies becomes dialogical, and can be used to examine the world of sport. There is a growing body of work on the culture of the fan, and on young people and rave, which has crossed into the study of the football crowd; we can relate this work to ideas derived from Bakhtin and from psychoanalytical theories. In their influential text *The Politics and Poetics of Transgression*, Peter Stallybrass and Allon White argued that in Britain, carnival was in decline from the seventeenth century onward.[5] Disruptive popular celebration was in retreat firstly from the more puritanical versions of Christianity which triumphed in the civil war of the 1640s, and secondly from the work discipline demanded from the machine-related work of the industrial revolution. Gradually fairs and circuses were marginalised, and quite literally driven to the periphery of working-class culture, the seaside resorts built for working-class recreation (places like Cleethorpes, Southend and Blackpool). In another influential book, *The Fall of Public Man*, Richard Sennett has argued that the nature of peoples' interaction in public changed, becoming quieter, more mutually respectful and less openly emotional (including less violent).[6] In particular, he claims that during the eighteenth century the 'masquerade' element of public life diminished. In the aristocracy and middle class, men ceased to wear make-up, flamboyantly coloured clothing, and wigs. Women of these classes continued to dress up, but were not encouraged to go out; the 'domestic sphere' became seen increasingly as 'woman's place'. These important aspects of culture, and in particular the stress on the material pleasures of the body and the pleasures of role-playing in public, were 'repressed'; but this repression has never been total, even for the middle class: Stallybrass and White, and Sennett, would agree with Bakhtin that traces of the carnival recur even in some ostentatiously 'high cultural' products, in literature, in music, and in art.

There were also strong traces of the carnivalesque in popular cultural forms such as music hall and pantomime (which unlike 'high' forms like opera, always allowed for a certain amount of public participation) and, of course, spectator sports in which (whatever the discipline displayed by the players) the crowd could and did behave drunkenly, abusively, and sometimes riotously. Popular spectator sporting occasions remain events during which the normal social rules are suspended; more daytime drinking than usual takes place; the circus comes to town, in the shape of the food and souvenir sellers who set up their stalls outside stadia; that very dialogical form of fantasy, gambling takes place, informally between friends as well as in official betting shops, and in a very limited way it turns the world upside down and makes the big winner king for a day.

There is another, complementary way of looking at these changes. Since the 1950s the so-called 'figurative sociology', the work of Norbert Elias and his followers, has become influential.[7] Elias has always been interested in sport, and his theories have always been applied to sport as much as to other aspects of society. The argument, like those of Bakhtin and Stallybrass and White, involves a particular interpretation of history. Here is an outline of the argument. Elias and friends argue that since the middle ages, western society has become more 'civilised', by which they mean better behaved, more temperate and less violent. Medieval sport was a violent part of a violent society: aristocratic tournaments, wild boar hunting, and quarterstaff fighting could all involve the serious injury, even death, of the participants. They claim that new forms of public discipline which were first practised at medieval courts spread down the social scale. First the ruling elite became less military and more polite and learned – in Britain castles were gradually replaced by magnificent, but indefensible, country houses, as the ruling classes gave up the civil wars and rebellions which had been routine in high politics before their apex, the seventeenth-century civil war. After this point, disagreements among gentlemen increasingly tended to take the form of parliamentary debate. At the same time, the gentlemanly elite began to set up the first nationally organised sports, cricket and horse racing. Then the middle classes sought to emulate the aristocracy and gentry, by gaining a classical education; sure enough the school system expanded massively during the nineteenth century, and sure enough the public schools and universities set up the next wave of nationally organised sports, the newly rationalised team games such as soccer and rugby. The values expressed in the ways these games were taught and played – values such as public restraint and fair play within the rules – then spread to those who took up the team sports with such enthusiasm, the skilled working class.

This growth of public restraint has necessarily meant changes in the general attitude to the body and its discipline, and many bodily activities formerly carried out in public have become increasingly private, hidden from the general view, and associated with shame and embarrassment: urination, defecation, and copulation being obvious examples. Sport is an example of this 'civilising process' in two ways. As well as providing a very necessary public arena for the display of aggressive confrontation, and for the display of public emotions, it displays, or demonstrates, the containing and disciplining of public violence. However violent they appear, Elias and followers argue, the new team sports show how high the threshhold of public toleration of resistance has risen since the time of the Roman gladiatorial arena, or the medieval tournament, in which people quite routinely killed others in front of cheering crowds.

These views can, I suggest, be taken as complementary; and yet in the differences between the Stallybrass and White position, and that of Elias and friends, we see one of the bigger problems of contemporary historical debate. Both positions are uncomfortable. Elias and company offer a vision of 'progress' that is deeply Eurocentric, elitist (claiming that change spreads from the top of the social scale downwards), and masculinised. Many people would argue that the replacement of public confrontation and uprising by parliamentary discourse has merely disempowered people. In other words, by following rules which have conveniently protected the lives and property of an elite, we have gravely damaged the potential for radical social change. The conservatism of this agenda is at its clearest when we consider the position of women in the Elias model. Their version of 'progress' is in many ways an apt description of the changing behaviour of men in the public sphere. Deaths caused by driving apart (and this is a very important exception), murder and serious injury inflicted by individuals on each other are no longer casual, routine, publicly tolerated occurences in Western Europe. But as Jennifer Hargreaves points out in her book on women in sport, violence by men against women remains commonplace; indeed, the incidence of reported rape and other domestic violence is on the increase.[8] Many women, especially those living in under-resourced working-class areas, are effectively denied a public sphere. As the father's movement involved in the backlash against the Child Support Agency indicates (in Britain, as recently in Australia and New Zealand) many men have no particular wish to increase their level of 'civilised' behaviour towards women. Fear and loathing will do quite nicely, thanks.

Fear and loathing is also present in the alternative account. Stallybrass and White, the carnival fans, argue that there has been repression of public display, including the display of public emotion. They see this as a bourgeois plot against people's real desires, joys, and interests. The implication is that casual murder, the misogynistic suppression of 'witchcraft', and animal-torturing games like bear-baiting and bull-running are alright, because unrepressed citizens enjoyed them during the middle ages. This, too, is uncomfortable. But is it even true that all popular culture is marginalised, peripheralised and repressed? Has the carnival really gone to the seaside and stayed there? Not really. In Britain, pantomimes and certain aspects of television and film humour (*Carry On* films, the television comedy *Bottom*) have provided some forms of continuity – and a very strange mixture of the repressed, the embarrassed, and the openly scatological they are too. Television is, of course, a crucial carrier of popular culture. Since the 1950s many aspects of carnival have been transcribed to popular television, with programmes in which studio audiences are present, and to a certain extent are there to participate in the proceedings rather than just sit, watch, and applaud when the floor manager tells them to. After-pub chat shows on Fridays and Saturdays and game shows are examples of television-transcribed carnival. Typically, these blend raucous humour with the opportunity for 'ordinary' people to turn their own worlds upside down and win money (e.g. in the virtually universal *Wheel of Fortune* format) or the chance of sex (the almost equally ubiquitous *Blind Date*). It is no coincidence that this type of populist programming is concentrated on Saturday evenings. Currently the Saturday format on British television includes the draw for that most carnivalesque inversion of personal fortune, the national lottery draw. It is no coincidence either that a programme of soccer highlights is usually included in this festival of popular culture.

But have television's relatively sanitised popular pleasures displaced the more dangerous joys of carnival in public? Here team sports remain important: because of the presence of the crowd, sporting occasions still have the potential for carnival's joyous anarchy. However, as the phenomenon of football hooliganism indicates, this can be problematic. Bakhtin, and Stallybrass and White, are commendably eager to criticise repressed bourgeois culture; but they have a regrettable tendency to romanticise opposing tendencies. The medieval or early modern carnival often involved moments of group definition through the exclusion of others (by the massacre of animals and people – the 'trial' and execution of cats and dogs, the lynching of alleged criminals, or the burning of alleged witches), and the misogyny, homophobia and racism commonly expressed in today's sports crowds dominated by white males indicates that the subversion of official discourses is not necessarily positive. Ask Eric Cantona.

However, while the moment of carnival may have seemed anarchic to its puritan opponents, it was in fact ordered; a reversal of existing power relations is still a hierarchy of power relations. Nevertheless, moments of control by the crowd (rather than its own officials) remain virtually intolerable both for the state and its discursive servants in the media. Most journalists, indeed, however radical their professed positions, tend to be monological by profession; they have no professional interest in non-journalists being given a voice in the public interpretation of events. The strong historic connection between the power of the crowd and moments of riot and rebellion, even of revolution, underlines the state's concern to curtail the freedom of public activity. There has often been an alliance between media, police, and the state in creating 'moral panics' as Stan Cohen called them.[9] These orchestrated panics are intended to produce counter-measures capable of undermining the apparently anarchic forces of the crowd. The latest manifestation of this will to control in Britain has produced the Criminal Justice Act of 1994, which, as I mention below, had as one of its targets control of the opposition to fox hunting. More generally, however, many of the provisions of this Draconian piece of legislation are directed against the most recent manifestation of carnival culture, the 'rave', a type of dance event held at large-scale parties. Raves involve illegal drugs, notably the inhibition-lowering MDMA ('Ecstasy'); they also involve a very dialogic, very strongly articulated, and very strongly spiritualised, alternative knowledge which combines aspects of the discourses of science and technology (in events whose musical and visual entertainments are created using computers) with a reworking of the romanticised anti-individualism of the drug experience, and a return to the values of paganism, especially in its celebration of aspects of 'nature'. All these aspects of rave culture are of concern to official discourses. The use of business machines such as computers (and modes of communication such as mobile phones) to set up and provide popular pleasures at rave events are as much a threat as the presence of large, unpoliced crowds. The combination of large numbers of people, new technologies and new knowledges is indeed subversive.

If rave is the most prominent ostensible target of this controlling legislation, it can as well be used against any other large gathering considered by the police to constitute a threat to public safety, including the football crowd, a gathering which has many times opposed the forces of law and order. Though this was not one of the Criminal Justice Act's explicit targets, there have been, as we shall see in chapter five, interesting connections between rave culture and the football crowd.

One very explicit target of the Criminal Justice Act (CJA), however, is a particular type of sporting crowd which like ravers uses a dialogic knowledge combining scientific, political, moral and spiritual discourses within an intense desire to change the future of sport. The CJA is quite explicitly directed against the activities of these people, the hunt saboteurs. 'Sabbing' is again a carnivalesque activity which aims to turn the world upside down through its opposition to a countryside sport still enthusiastically supported by the monarchy, aristocracy and wealthy upper middle class. It is also a sport itself, with its own rules, its own exploration of time and space, and a fiercely competitive edge; the immediate goal of the sport, on a daily basis, is to prevent the hunt from killing foxes (or other animal prey such as deer or mink). The CJA intends to frustrate the activities of the followers of this unofficial sport by creating a new offence of 'aggravated trespass'. It therefore intends to reverse a legal gain which was forced by carnival-like action. In the 1930s the crowd loosened the trespass laws after a series of mass trespasses on shooting estates in the north of England. The 1932 Rights of Way Act and 1935 Access to Mountains Act meant that thereafter land-owners have had to be more responsive to the needs of ramblers.[10] In the 1990s, it seems, this comparative freedom has been reversed in the interests of, among other things, the traditional sport of hunting.

Hunt saboteurs, then, are both representatives of one aspect of traditional sport – the carnivalesque – and in another respect the opponents of traditional sport – the hunt, the legacy of the game laws, the 'traditional' life of the countryside in which animals such as foxes are the enemies of farmers. It could even be argued that the sabbers are the heirs of the puritans who combatted traditional bloodsports in the seventeenth century; or that they use carnival culture against aspects of the carnival tradition. For there can be no doubt that traditional sports were nasty, brutish, and for all that they were enjoyed by the aristocracy, many were also deeply popular.

Warfare, Hunting, and Gender

Contests between individuals and teams were usually very violent, often leading to severe injury, sometimes to death: though the violence was never the ostensible purpose of the competition, confrontations between villages had something of the atmosphere of civil war. Quarterstaff fighting and wrestling involved people as representatives, or champions, of their communities, while in village football, as with similar games like shinty in Scotland and hurling in Ireland, whole communities became participants. Unsurprisingly, some commentators have claimed that the origins of sport are to be found in a ritual celebration of warfare, or a preparation for war. The language of sports journalism is often military in derivation, and even the signature tunes of sports programmes are usually military marches. Certainly the ancient Greeks were aware of the connection, and one form of sport actually encouraged by the state in medieval Britain was archery, which has obvious military uses: in 1541 a law was passed making archery practise compulsory and banning football.[11] Football then became 'militarised' in its turn. The founding statement issued by the Scottish Football Association in 1873 makes the connections between sport, war and masculinity (and capitalism) quite plain: football was to be encouraged 'to produce in the inhabitants of our native land a bold, athletic, and manly race . . . to preserve the Scottish bone and muscle which has so often proven its worth in many a hard-fought field of war, and of industry, throughout the world'.[12]

Two Olympic events are specifically military in origin. The modern pentathlon (fencing, shooting, swimming, cross-country running and riding) was first contested at the 1912 Olympics. It is based on a scenario in which a despatch rider has to take a message through enemy lines, facing various perils along the way. The biathlon (cross-country skiing and rifle shooting), introduced in 1960, is a direct product of the Cold War and the potential confrontation between Soviet and NATO forces in northern Europe – it is a sporting version of the soldier's training routine for warfare in snow. Some military-sporting connections are rather less plausible. In 1994 the British Ministry of Defence was trying to argue the continuing connection between fox hunting, the skills of horsemanship, and the training of cavalry officers (for ceremonial duties – most of their military skills will, even in an age of defence cuts, presumably be exercised from the control tower of a tank rather than on horseback!). However, the MOD only subsidised the presence of cavalry *officers* at hunts while on duty, while denying the same privilege to horse riders in the other ranks, who might need the same skills in parades, if not battles.[13]

This military connection is sometimes used in turn in an explanation of the historic exclusion of women from all kinds of sporting activity. While it is true that most military cultures have been exclusively masculine (there are important exceptions such as pre-Christian Celtic cultures, the army of Dahomey in nineteenth-century West Africa, and, of course, the legendary Amazons), it is hard to sustain this claim in detail. Women's participation in sport is a historic variable; in Europe it seems to have been at its lowest during the nineteenth century; there is a great deal of evidence that there was more female participation in sport in pre-industrial Britain (and also in France) than there was in the nineteenth or early twentieth centuries. The systematic exclusion of women from the public sphere which was consolidated early in the nineteenth century can be seen as another legacy of the Puritan attack on traditional sports and the carnivalesque expression of the powers and pleasures of the body. Paradoxically, one of the few sports routinely practised by middle-class women during the nineteenth century was archery, a competition with very clear military connections – archery was considered respectable because it did not encourage the display of the female body in movement. Target shooting using smallbore rifles, another military-derived exercise requiring stillness rather than movement, is one of the few areas of sport in which women routinely compete directly against men – though, depressingly, they are not yet permitted to do so at the Olympic Games. Women also compete against men, and often excel over them, at another of these quasi-military contests, the three-day event. While the female eventer's body does indeed move, the prime mover in this exercise is the horse; the rider, apart from the (important) act of balance, has to become the animal's mind for the duration of the contest.

As with ancient Rome, there were also common popular sports in pre-industrial Britain which revolved around another kind of violence, the torturing and killing of animals. Another reasonable proposal about the origins of sport claims its lineage from hunting. 'Field sports', involving hunting, shooting and fishing, are still practised throughout the world by people who do not actually need the fur and flesh of the animals, birds and fish they hunt. Team sports like, say, ice hockey may seem a long way from the hunt, and a long way from contemporary field sports like deerstalking – or even clay pigeon shooting, where the descent from hunting may be more obvious, and where the size and shape of the target (the clay) are similar to that of the hockey puck. But the organising of a project around a goal, achieved through team work and discipline, were important in the capturing and killing of large animals – as they were in warfare. This connection with hunting, again, may help to explain the insistence which can still be heard in some quarters that sport is an essentially masculine activity. It is often argued that the division between the 'masculine' hunting, and the 'feminine' duty of domestic food processing and preparation, is one of the earliest stages in the formation of patriarchal societies, in which men are in political control because they are in control of all public activity. Sport, it can be argued, symbolises that continuing power relationship.

Once again, this is too simple an opposition, though it does offer some insights. Women's involvement in the ritualised public celebration of the outcome of the hunt is clear from both historical and contemporary anthropological evidence; we must remember that there was more female involvement in the public sphere before the early nineteenth century stress on the importance of the domestic sphere for women. No doubt from that moment on the increasing masculinisation of work, with its supporting ideology of the notion that the man of the ideal household is the 'breadwinner', and the woman the (house)wife and mother, operated against the involvement of women in public life; and this division can be seen as a 'civilised', highly abstract version of a world in which men go out hunting and women stay at home preparing food and looking after the children. This model would imply that at the moment when men are no longer able to function satisfactorily as sole breadwinners, then women will enter the public sphere – including the sporting arena.

This seems to have happened. In Britain, the massive struggle for female suffrage achieved its first successes during the first world war, in which the male military/hunting/sporting connection had denied men the role of family-sustaining breadwinner (partly by taking them away from hearth, home and factory floor for four years; partly by killing, throughout Europe, nine million of those on active service, and wounding to incapacity millions more). During the war years men left the workplace in such large numbers that women were recruited to do jobs which men had previously monopolised. They also played the sports men had played; in Britain women's football became a popular spectator sport, and it remained popular until pressure from the male football authorities shut down the women's leagues in the 1920s. But nothing was quite the same again. After the slaughter of the trenches, though many men returned to work, many did not; 'shell shock', male hysteria, was diagnosed alongside the more visible wounds of the conflict.[14]

Thus began the long crisis of masculinity which has marked the twentieth century; and thus began the long narrative of gender-differentiated progress in sports, as women's rate of achievement has risen faster than men's, in an interesting parallel with Western men's declining relative earnings. This is a long story, which continues. Since the 1950s, the ideal of the male breadwinner cheerfully servicing a household with a wife and children not in gainful employment has become unsustainable. Many women from middle-class households now work full-time through what they and their partners perceive to be necessity. The current generation in the USA is, it is claimed, the first which cannot expect to achieve a higher standard of living than its parents. There may still be Marxists who would claim that this is because of the immutable laws of capitalism, i.e. that the rate of profit is in long-term decline; though it could as easily be argued that global capital simply has no need to dissipate profit in payment of first world wages, but is giving people elsewhere in the world a higher standard of living. Whatever, this economic disappointment has been another reason for the crisis in Western masculinity; it is not coincidental that the gradual increase in women's public economic activity, as potential equals of their partners, has occurred at the same time that women's sporting activity has increased so rapidly. But as I pointed out through the example of the *Sun* newspaper's construction of Sally Gunnell as Essex Girl, the advances in women's public activity have been matched by male fear and hatred, a 'backlash' against feminist advances, and a revival in some quarters of the belief that women should not come first, or race at all; that they should be mothers before anything else.

Power relations between men and women in the West are currently, as ever no doubt, in a state of flux. The much-publicised 'backlash' (which undoubtedly exists, and can be seen in the intensity of the debates over abortion in the USA) has a very interesting complement in the idea of 'genderquake'.[15] British girls are currently doing better than boys in all aspects of the school curriculum; girls leaving school have a far clearer idea of their future career prospects and the training they need in order to achieve them. Theorists of education are casting around for explanations of this male 'underperformance', whose impact in the medium term will be most interesting, in sports and their role in society as in everything else. Meanwhile, as the astonishing performances of Chinese women swimmers and middle distance runners at recent world championships has shown, women's sporting performance continues to improve at a far greater rate than men's.

The Boundaries of Humanity

If gendered power relations are gradually being undermined, there is one set of power relations, expressed through sport, which has been if anything reinforced through the twentieth century. In ritualised hunting sports, or other public entertainments such as bullfighting, human societies have expressed their power over animals. It can be argued that this demonstration of power is used as a ritualised demonstration of the difference between organised human society and 'nature'. By treating animals in an 'inhumane' way, people signal to each other that *they* are human, and exempt from this kind of treatment.

This left, as it still leaves, domesticated animals, especially dogs, in an ambivalent position – as the phrase 'a dog is man's best friend' testifies. Dogs provide a mediating point between the animal and the human. Since the first wolf was persuaded to hunt alongside humans in return for indoor accommodation and food during cold weather, dogs have been altered by their human owners, bred for various purposes such as the hunting of other animals, including their lupine ancestors. They have also been bred to compete against each other in the very basic sport of greyhound racing. Their adaptation for use in hunting and racing makes dogs one of the earliest examples of sporting technology; but they also have a very important role in the policing of the human/animal boundary. As law enforcers, dogs constantly revive the notion that those who transgress are outlaws, and therefore animals themselves; and may, as the saying goes, be hunted down like dogs. By dogs.

The associated type of policing, as the recent growth in the genre of 'true crime' television indicates, is a game, a sporting drama. What we have in many of the true crime reconstructions is human-hunting. There are televised car chases, or grossly dramatised reconstructions of crimes followed by appeals for witnesses, and so on. In all these programmes the object is a hunt for someone who is outside the law, and therefore fair game, or 'vermin', in the same way as foxes are said to be fair game by those who like hunting them. As in fox-hunting or hare-coursing, there is nothing inevitable about the outcome of the chase – which is why the comparison with sports is so apt; in other words, the object of the hunt may escape.

True crime television's dramatisation of the hunt is indicative of the real ethical problems which arise when it is decided that certain categories of people are 'unnatural', or 'inhuman' or 'subhuman', therefore animal and that it is therefore permissible to hunt, capture, torture and

destroy them as animals. Witches, homosexuals, Christians, heretics, Jews, and black people have all been
characterised and victimised in this way at various times.
The relationship between, for example, the public
execution of witches (common through much of seventeenth century Europe), and the public rituals of local or
international sporting contests should at least be pon-
dered. In each case there are winners, acclaimed by the
public as one of themselves (the accuser or trial judge, the
jury, the matchwinners), and losers (the accused and
convicted witch, the match losers), rejected by the public as
not one of themselves.

The Scapegoat and the Champion

The loser is as important as the winner; societies seem to
need scapegoats, individuals or groups of people on whom
they can transfer their fears, guilts and hatreds. Such
individuals are often mythologised in religion, and in
contemporary society through the star system in film,
music and the arts, and in sport. This scapegoat need not
be an outsider, but can be one of their own, especially if
she or he fails to uphold accepted behavioural standards
and/or fails in a representative contest. The reaction of
supporters to the defeat of their chosen team or players
can be very hostile: they affirm their collective identity but
in refusing their champion her or his previous status, they
excommunicate him or her; the defeated player is no
longer 'one of us': to lose is a sign of unnaturalness.

In sport, as in other aspects of popular culture such as
film and music, the star system becomes the focus of public
attention. Film stars and musicians are under the public
gaze; they too are worshipped as champions, and vilified,
even excommunicated, when they fail or are seen publicly
to transgress moral or other social norms. Whatever the
patterns of their actual lives, writings about stars (film stars
or rock musicians as much as sports performers) portray
them as scapegoats and/or champions. They are constructed as isolated, misunderstood, vulnerable individuals, and as prophets with unique gifts of insight and
ability; and, often simultaneously, they are demonised as

drug-sodden misfits, unable to live with their own gifts. The Faust legend (the story of a man who sells his soul to the devil in order to achieve his desires on earth) lurks closely behind these stories of people who transgress in order to achieve greatness – especially those who do so through drugtaking. This applies as much to musicians like Charlie Parker or Janis Joplin (both of whom died young, partly due to an excess of internal chemical redesign) as it does to athletes like Ben Jonson (stripped of his 1988 Olympic 100 metre title) or Diego Maradonna (sent home from the 1994 soccer World Cup) after they had tested positive for performance-enhancing drugs.

This may seem to be merely an official demonisation. The illegal drugs industry is policed, and users are 'busted' by the law, 'dried out' by the medical profession and psychotherapists, and so on. Athletes are tested by officials, their blood and urine samples then processed by white-coated scientists who work within the severely monological discourses of applied science – the laboratory testers see themselves as purveyors of unvarnished and irrefutable truths. And yet there is a popular dimension to this process. As I mentioned above, 'policing' is part of a very common series of popular narratives, including police and detective series and 'true crime'. This 'theatre of control' is itself a form of policing, in this case the arbiter of the acceptable and the natural body. Through its presentation by the media, the control, and sometimes the expulsion, of athletes who have taken drugs, becomes part of a public spectacle of normalisation, which sets up the righteous non-drug-using heroes on one hand, and the unrighteous scapegoats on the other. It is therefore part of the world of spectator sport. The crowd, as we have seen, can become the agent of carnival, a world turned upside down in which those normally outside the law can direct it. We have also seen how this kind of intervention can produce public fears, which can in turn lead to hostile legislation. The moment of carnival can therefore be seen as oppositional or subversive. But crowd does not equal carnival, in this sense: in many cases, as in the wide public agreement that drugtaking is morally wrong, and that drugtaking in sport is a form of cheating, the participation of the crowd is deeply conservative. There is a wide public acceptance that the body has certain limits, and that these limits must not be exceeded: that to take drugs is a sign of unnaturalness, inhumanity. Again, sport polices and ritualises the bounds of the natural – though whether this situation can withstand the increasing deconstruction of the 'natural' at the nodal point of the body itself is a moot point, to which I return in Chapter Four.

At present, however, these rituals of exclusion or inclusion remain with us, and one of their most powerful roles remains the policing of the human/animal boundary. Sports involving animals as victims, such as fox-hunting in Britain and bullfighting in Spain and Latin America, remain popular, if controversial. In some parts of the world, indeed, there is growing pressure to end the preservation of some species and to reintroduce hunting. Deer, and even bears in parts of the Northern United States and Canada, have been preserved from hunting; therefore their populations have increased – partly in the case of deer because of the absence of their predator, wolves, which have been systematically hunted from most of the continent; the controversial reintroduction of the wolf into northern American states may reverse this trend if farmers don't shoot them all. At present the large numbers of hungry animals annoy farmers and towns-people by destroying crops and, in the case of bears (powerful animals quite capable of killing humans), also invade towns looking for food; thus they are candidates for a renewal of the boundaries between humanity and nature which hunting sports have always policed, and for a renewal of the patriarchal system which hunting has often guaranteed. If bear-hunting returns to the United States, it will be part of the backlash.

The Boundary of the Natural

Hunting sports also clearly explore, and demarcate, human territorial boundaries. This applies to virtually all sports, but in rather different ways. Village cricket matches on 'the green' underline the sense of the public space as the centre of the community. The territorial disputes over the small green spaces of the football ground are well known, as are the occasionally violent confrontations for possession of this urban territory. But possession of space is perhaps most clearly at stake in field sports. Landowners shoot 'their' estates or fish 'their' stretches of rivers; fox-hunts are local in origin, and even now, when their members are likely to be incoming commuters rather than local people, keep to within boundaries agreed with other packs – these boundaries are usually derived from parishes or landed estates. More recent competitive sports like orienteering and fell-running also allow the policing of boundaries, the establishing of a sense of place within the athletes' narratives of regional and national identity. Some sports, on the other hand, deliberately transgress these boundaries. Rambling became a political issue in the Britain of the 1930s as people from the towns fought to gain access to landed estates which were until then reserved for hunting or shooting. In a more general sense, mountaineering, backpacking and other uncompetitive but highly skilled country activities allow non-landowners to appropriate for themselves places, views, which do not 'belong' to, and cannot be seen by, anyone not prepared to undergo the fierce physical efforts necessary for these activities. The backpacker can enter the wilderness and live for a while without human contact in a landscape which has not yet been transformed by human activity, can therefore temporarily deny her or his humanity, in a reversal of the policing of the human/natural boundary which is so important to most field sports.[16]

Whatever their origins, activities involving the policing and ritualised control of nature were universal in pre-industrial England. Bears, bulls and badgers were 'baited', tied to posts and attacked by dogs. Cocks, and dogs, were made to fight each other, dogs were set on rats, hares were coursed (caught, set free and chased by dogs) and hares, rabbits, wild boar, wolves, foxes and otters were hunted with people, sometimes on horseback, leading packs of dogs trained by careful breeding to follow and kill these particular prey. The larger and more dangerous animals, bears, wild boar, and wolves were hunted to extinction. These traditional activities were not, as is sometimes suggested, played in a world without commerce. Money was made from sport in pre-industrial England; by the eighteenth century there were professional wrestlers, prizefighters, jockeys and cricketers, and an informal 'circus' circuit of venues, fairs and so on, for their performance; and as with most sport throughout history, fighting, cricket and racing were accompanied by gambling. Money or goods would be bet on the outcome of a contest, or the time taken for victory, or the performances of individuals. All this remains important in most sporting activity today, adding to the excitement of both spectators and players.

The Boundary of Class

These pre-industrial pursuits, notably the 'field sports' of coursing and hunting, were on the cusp of a characteristic and continuing division within British society: the division of class. To oversimplify, Puritans were by and large middle-class, the followers of professions with adequate earnings, rather than aristocrats with plenty of inherited, land-based money and legal protection, or the poorer lower classes. Sporting needs, desires and opportunities were differently distributed among these social groups. From the early years of Norman-French rule over the English (after 1066), when the Normans had created large areas of depopulated wasteland on which to hunt, by clearing people from the land (areas such as the New Forest in Hampshire), there had been laws protecting the rights of the rich and powerful to hunt certain species of animals and birds specified as 'game' – the Game Laws.[17] These privileges were held quite literally at the expense of the poor and even of local farmers and landowners, who were not allowed to hunt these animals, and could even be punished by death for doing so. Hunting deer and rabbits, and shooting pheasants and partridge, remained the prerogative only of those with great landed wealth, and their guests, until the 1830s, when all animals became the property of those on whose land they were found. Meanwhile, there were bitter, often violent disputes between rich hunters (and their gamekeepers) and poor 'poachers', many of whom hunted for a living, illegally selling game to poulterers and other caterers in towns.

The wealthy hunters had no need to hunt for a living, and they made the sale of game illegal: thus only they and their friends could (legally) even taste the animals and birds they destroyed. This very stark opposition between hunting for love and for money (or subsistence), based on class difference, was carried over into the more general concept of the 'amateur', who takes part in sporting activity for the love of it rather than for professional reasons.

The idea of the amateur remains important in contemporary debate about sport. But the concept was always an ideal rather than a rule, and it does not necessarily mean that no money was involved in sport; some 'amateurs', such as cricketers W.G. Grace and Archie MacLaren, were paid very generous expenses; as with popular sport, most aristocratic sport was the site of gambling. The word 'professional' has also encompassed meanings which are rather different in sport. In most circumstances, the word professional signifies middle-class educational status, with the ability to practise being conditional on examination success and the license of some professional body such as the British Medical Association. The sporting professional, on the other hand, will be a skilled worker, whether a 'representative' team player or a freelance 'circus' performer such as a snooker player. While athletes are trained, they are subject to apprenticeship schemes rather than higher education degrees and professional licenses (though their coaches will usually be examined and licensed on the middle-class professional model).

The continuing linguistic legacy of this pre-industrial culture clash over the meaning of sport underlines an important counter to the very broad claims that modern sport is nothing like pre-industrial sport; that the differences are far stronger than the similarities. The amateur/professional debate occurred in the seventeenth and eighteenth centuries, and reappeared at the end of the nineteenth. Even in the late twentieth century, as television and advertising exert what appears to be a stranglehold over public sports and therefore change their meaning, the amateur/professional debate is still with us – and it is *still* fundamentally about the difference between those who value participation 'for its own sake' (and can afford to) and those who wish, either as agents, administrators or athletes, to make their living from sport.

Class Interaction and the Emergence of Modern Sport

The reform of the game laws, in the 1830s, took place at a crucial time for the future of British sport, because of the change which was taking place in the power structure of the state. It was the 1830s, in fact, which saw the consolidation of the rise to power of the business class which was finally allowed an entry into Parliament after the 1832 Reform Act. This class had two contradictory impulses: firstly, to impose its own cultural norms on society as a whole (which meant attacking aristocratic culture, and attempting to reform working-class culture), and secondly, to become accepted by the aristocracy – including acceptance into existing aristocratic culture. The newly powerful middle class who gained entry into parliamentary politics at this time were in some ways the spiritual heirs of puritanism, with a distrust of any kind of popular entertainment. During the nineteenth century many remaining popular sports, especially those involving cruelty to animals, and the gambling associated with them, were suppressed (or rather driven underground; dog-fighting and badger-baiting remain on the illegal fringes of British male working-class culture, and even in 1991 legislation against the American pit bull terrier, a breed of fighting dog, could be interpreted as another attack by middle-class puritans on popular sporting culture).

There was, however, no revolution which swept away all other cultures. The middle class did not achieve complete political dominance either over the working-class or over the aristocracy; working class sport and gambling remained in compressed form, in the semi-professional athletic contests known as 'pedestrianism' for instance. Meanwhile, a compromise was reached between middle-class and aristocratic cultural values. While some forms of aristocratic culture, such as public drunkenness, duelling, and gambling at card games, also came under attack during and after the 1830s, aristocratic animal torture remained legal. This was partly a direct trade-off for middle-class infiltration into aristocratic sport: fox-hunting, shooting and horse racing became more open to middle-class ownership and participation; horse racing remained virtually the only legal site of gambling, and continued to employ professional jockeys, who were always, as they remain, the outstanding riders – though there are still amateur riders, especially at the lower levels of the sport.

Another aristocratic leisure site, the gentleman's club, became the model for the social organisation of virtually all sporting activity involving the middle classes. The club as an institution protected amateurism. In the case of horse racing, the established ruling body was already a club, the Jockey Club, and cricket was ruled by the Marylebone Cricket Club or MCC; while the ruling bodies of soccer and rugby union were clubs in all but name, self-perpetuating oligarchies of the high-born. County cricket clubs, and suburban tennis and golf clubs, also used the members' club model, offering people playing and non-playing subscriptions to become in effect joint owners of the facilities. The committees of these organisations policed entry to membership, on grounds of class, gender and race. The association of suburban tennis and the 'polite society' of the white middle class continues. Tennis in particular, as a sport which girls were allowed, even encouraged to play from early in the twentieth century, became the site for sexual selection. This increased the element of class policing (as middle-class parents had no wish for their daughters to meet working-class men, however athletically gifted); the resultant association of tennis and middle-class flirtation can be put forward as one of the reasons for the continuing 'failure' of British tennis to produce international champions. Tennis had become a leisure pursuit rather than a competitive sport; a profession dominated by amateurs, in which the only place for the 'professional' was as a servant of the club, available to give advice on members' techniques. The situation in most provincial golf clubs is similar.

A rather different compromise was effected over team sports, most of which in both aristocratic and popular forms had been thoroughly violent – older boys at Rugby school, for instance, were permitted to wear steel-shod boots to 'hack' for the ball in the scrum, despite the effects of this on the younger boys. The rules of association and rugby football curbed this kind of violence (without altogether preventing it) and ordered these games into closer boundaries of time and space. In both the new team sports and the established team game, cricket (which like racing had involved paid professionals from the eighteenth century onwards, though in this case there were also many successful amateur players), gambling on the result was replaced by competition for trophies or medals (not money), and with an accompanying belief that the love of the game, and participation in it, were enough to give pleasure to participant and spectator alike.

The reordering is seen at its starkest and most dramatic in the case of boxing. This 'noble and manly art' emerged, Phoenix-like, from the ashes of prizefighting, in which sport was at its most atavistic. Like cricket and horse racing, prizefighting had been a commercialised public sport in the eighteenth century. Two men fought in a ring, usually with bare fists, until one of them was no longer capable of putting up any resistance. The contests could last for hours; in most cases both winner and loser were badly injured. Large sums of money were won and lost on the outcome of these contests, which were patronised, often organised, by aristocrats, and contested by working-class men. In the middle of the nineteenth century, this activity was banned – and again went underground: several British championship fights took place abroad. For a generation, legal fistfighting disappeared from Britain. However, late in the nineteenth century two aristocrats, the Earl of Lonsdale and the Marquis of Queensberry, helped to found a club at Covent Garden in London at which the rules of boxing evolved – with padded gloves, an agreed number of three-minute rounds, and ringside medical supervision. Though the most popular fighters were professionals, gambling was again de-emphasised; boxing was soon being taught in boys' schools and youth clubs as a respectable amateur sport. The new arrangement is still known as the Queensberry rules, and British boxing champions still fight for the Lonsdale belt; though the important thing about the club was that its membership was largely drawn from the respectable middle class. The club's committee controlled both the professional and amateur game. Two generations after the puritanical middle class had entered Parliament and banned many violent sports, its heirs sat in a Covent Garden club, wearing dinner suits, and watched men punch each other in the head.[18]

Modern Sport: Rationalisation Theory

So this taming of violent competitive sport carries with it contradictory echoes of Puritanism. The use of the word 'Puritanism' here is not, of course, to claim that all sport was approved of by organised evangelical Christianity (which became open to team sports but was and is still hostile to boxing, for instance), but to emphasise the seriousness with which sport was treated in schools and universities, and teams associated with churches and Sunday schools. It became a mode of bodily discipline to complement the mental disciplines of religious observance and education. The sociologist of sport Allen Guttmann has claimed convincingly that 'modern' sport has evolved into a routinised and bureaucratised form.[19] Here was discipline and restraint, where before there was the excess and disorder of Carnival; the discipline of the dedicated training of the individual body and of specific role-playing within teams, and the further discipline of obedience to the rules and those who enforce them, the umpires, referees and the bureaucrats in Boards of Control who policed and occasionally remade the rules. Drawing on the work of sociologists Talcott Parsons and Max Weber, Guttmann identified seven facets of contemporary sport:

1 Secularism
2 Equality of opportunity to compete, and in the conditions of competition
3 Specialisation of roles
4 Rationalisation
5 Bureaucratic organisation
6 Quantification
7 The quest for records

These claims have become so important and influential in the sociological analysis of sport that they repay careful attention. I shall offer a brief commentary on each proposition, which will qualify Guttmann's position, before briefly considering some other theoretical treatments of sport. But it is worth reiterating that this analysis has become influential because it is in many ways convincing.

1. Secularism

By this Guttmann claims that much of the ritual which societies used to associate with sport has been removed. Sports and games in, for example, ancient Greece and pre-Columbus Mexico, were constituent parts of acts of religious worship in the same way that certain sorts of music are associated with religious worship today. They were associated with specific ceremonies, times and places, and could not be performed otherwise. It is difficult today to find any such direct connection between sports and religion. While Guttmann concedes that to some extent sports have themselves become a 'secular faith', he insists that there has been a qualitative change: 'We do not run in order that the earth may be more fertile. We till the earth, or work in our factories and offices, so that we have time to play'.[20]

While this is true as far as it goes, it seems, like much of Guttmann's argument, to be an excessively rationalist view of the sports process. The churches played an important part in the spread of team games in the late-nineteenth century, hoping that healthy minds in healthy bodies would worship God with increased vigour. Many British professional soccer teams, such as Southampton and Aston Villa, began as representatives of local churches. The Catholic church in Ireland supported the late nineteenth century revival of Gaelic sports, and ran its own Gaelic football and hurling leagues until the 1950s. The Catholic church in Italy, meanwhile, cultivated its parishioners through the support of professional cycling, promoting one particular cyclist, Gino Bartali, as the hero of the faith and the enemy of communism. When a few days after an attempted communist coup Bartali won the

1948 Tour de France, the church presented this triumph as a victory for Christian democracy.[21] More generally, the Victorian stress on the healthy mind in the healthy body was directly expressed in the concept of 'muscular christianity' which is to be found in much of the writing of the novelist and Anglican priest Charles Kingsley – see for example *Yeast* (1851). Muscular christianity is a crucial component of arguably the most important of all sporting texts, Thomas Hughes's novel *Tom Brown's Schooldays* (1856), with its invocation of rugby football and cricket as embodiments of physical and moral virtue. The connection is not dead. The current Anglican bishop of Liverpool, the Right Reverend David Sheppard, is a former England cricket international who among other achievements took two Test centuries off the Australians.

Of course religion, sport and the state are not always easy bedfellows. Many athletes pray as they enter the field of play. When the Czechoslovakian soccer forward Petras opened his side's scoring in the 1970 World Cup finals, he knelt on the field and crossed himself – a religious gesture in direct oppposition to his state's self-proclaimed atheism. In Islam, any female participation in public sporting events, like anything else which exposes the female body to the male gaze, can be treated as heresy. Hassima Boulmerka was forced to leave Morocco after her victory in the 1,500 metres at the 1991 World Athletic Championships. But female athletic performance *has* been tolerated in Islam, under certain conditions. In 1993 an Islamic Women's Games was held in Tehran, behind closed doors, and like the Heratic games in ancient Greece open to female spectators (and athletes) only.[22] In those parts of the world which have most successfully resisted the processes of secularisation, the combination of a healthy mind and a healthy body can be recognised, and some theologically correct form of sporting activity remains possible.

A simple reaction to Guttmann's claims of secularisation would be that his deeply rationalist argument is itself a fantasy: the fantasy of modernism. Rather like the Elias version of history, this is a positivist, Eurocentric view of change. The fantasy resides in the claim that since some point in history (the usual starting points are the fifteenth-century Renaissance, the eighteenth-century Enlightenment, and the nineteenth-century spread of Darwin's theory of the evolution of species) scientific rationality has become the norm, the most important ideology through which we see the world. In fact spirituality is far from dead, and sport is an instance of its survival: sport is not just a 'secular faith' but a religion, the object of many people's worship. Through this worship they can express their obsessions, fears and desires in exactly the same way as the churchgoer. An entirely rational view of sport has no place for its most important current embodiment of the sacral, the star system, and cannot see the spiritual importance of the sporting manifestations of the champion and the scapegoat. Both roles are crucial to religion: the stories of the life of Christ, paraded through the streets of Jerusalem as a hero but vilified by the same public a week later; or Krishna, the aspect of the Hindu deity who is represented as blue because he has taken on all the poisons of the world; these are played over and over again by the rise and fall of champions worshipped in victory, rejected in defeat, socially necessary in both. The star system is reworking very important human narratives. 'Secularisation' has not disturbed these at all. Sport is more than merely secular faith.

The Palestinians who murdered Israeli athletes at the Munich Olympics of 1972 took this view, their spokesman claiming 'We recognise that sport is the modern religion of the world . . . so we decided to use the Olympics, the most sacred ceremony of this religion, to make the world pay attention to us'.[23] Sport is not and never has been purely secular; its continued carrying of the sacral implies a strong qualification of Guttmann's thesis.

2. *Equality of opportunity to compete, and in the conditions of competition*

Guttmann argues that ancient sport tended to be exclusive. Only people from certain social groups were allowed to compete – entry was restricted to citizens in the case of the Greeks, while in Rome the citizens were perfectly happy to sit around and watch their more routinely deadly entertainments, making professional gladiators, captured warriors, heretics, or their slaves, compete to kill each other.

Many societies have excluded people from access to sporting competition on grounds of class. In sixteenth-century England, the game of bowls was forbidden to those without land worth the considerable sum of £100 per year. In nineteenth-century England, amateur athletics, tennis and rowing clubs had membership rules which routinely prevented the skilled working class, whether or not they were amateur, from applying for membership. The rules of the Amateur Athletic Association, founded in 1867, stated quite plainly that 'an amateur is a person who has never competed in an open competition or for public money or for admission money . . . or is a mechanic artisan or labourer'.[24] Gender has been another common point of exclusion; there were men-only and women-only Games meetings in ancient Greece; women had to fight to gain entry to the modern Olympics, competing in a limited range of events first in 1908, and have fought since for the right to compete in the full range of events. Skin colour has also been used to restrict both participation and observation. Apartheid South Africa banned 'mixed-race' teams or leagues in any sport, and also segregated audiences (and was itself then segregated from international competition); black Americans were not permitted to play major league baseball until the 1940s.

Guttmann argues that in most parts of the world category restrictions of this kind are disappearing. He stresses that equality of opportunity is an important ideal, and that the administrators of many sports make every effort to ensure its realisation. In boxing, competitors are grouped according to body weight. No bantamweight would last five minutes with a heavyweight, but two bantamweights are permitted to slug it out in an equal contest to find the true champion. Generally, the Olympic Games welcomes participant athletes from all over the world, with no restrictions according to nationality, or ethnicity, or sexual preference. Most sports are now run for women as well as men. The rules of the competition, including the playing conditions, time allowed, number of attempts to jump and so on, are the same for each contestant; furthermore, officials are present to ensure that this is the case, to prevent foul play or unfair advantage gained by drug use.

All very laudable. But these are ideals, and they are a very partial, very constructed set of ideals. Genuine equality of opportunity to compete is a virtual impossibility. Major athletics contests organised along international lines restrict the possibilities for those who come from poorer countries, without the technical or coaching facilities of the wealthier nations. Well aware of this, the International Olympic Committee spends some of its vast wealth in trying to address this problem, building facilities in poorer countries, and offering scholarships for promising athletes to attend college in the USA. But there are wider problems which should be addressed. Gendered events seem an increasingly artifical way of dividing the sporting world. In some types of contest, such as long distance swimming, women are already the equals of men. If we took the example of boxing or weightlifting, both of which group contestants according to weight, and applied it to high jumping or pole vaulting, athletes would be divided into categories of height. In this case women could compete against men on equal terms – indeed, they would probably win the majority of contests. This raises a related problem. The human body will, it seems, expand to fit the limits of the category, where such exist. The average height of the basketball player and rugby forward continues to increase; it has already gone well beyond the point where such people look like ordinary human beings. Against a team of seven-footers, there is no way for a team of six-foot basketball players to compete.

This leads to the fundamental point: it is precisely the opportunity to compete which is important. The rapid increase in sporting opportunities for the disabled, and for older people, are a very positive direction in sports provision. But no one is interested in hobbling the biggest and fastest in the interests of an entirely spurious notion of equality of performance. The exception is in horse racing, where the handicap system attempts to equalise differences by making consistent winners carry weights. But this exists for one purpose only: to make betting less reliable and more interesting, and therefore to keep the punters and their money rolling in to betting shops.

3. Specialisation of roles

This is another notion which owes a lot to Max Weber's ideas about the growth of rationality – with a nod in the direction of Karl Marx's ideas about the division of labour. And, of course, there is much to be said for the argument. Village football was a game of all against all, without specialist strikers, midfield players, defenders or goal-keepers, or even a defined playing area, just a lot of people, two goals and a pig's bladder (the ball). Furthermore, the concept of sporting excellence in the individual was not specialised either. The ideal was the all-rounder; and in such a figure as Squire Osbaldeston (1786–1866) the ideal was very nearly realised. The squire ran, rode, drove, hunted, shot, played billiards and cricket, boxed and duelled. He had a high opinion of his capabilities at each activity, and was prepared to back it, to the extent that he bet his way through a considerable fortune (one calculation is that his high estimate of his own sporting prowess cost him over £300,000).[25] In India there was the similar figure of the Rajah of Patilda, Rajinder Singh (1872–1900), a sporting virtuoso who excelled at polo and tennis; ran races; hunted cheetah and stuck pigs; played cricket; and in order to create a successful cricket team, he hired the best Indian players regardless of religion, and brought in some of the best English professionals of the time to coach them.[26]

But although this polyathletic ideal is preserved in contemporary athletic events such as the pentathlon and modern pentathlon, the growth of professionalism, late in the nineteenth century, tended to focus performers' energies on one sport, and increasingly on one particular position within team games. It was soon realised that each sport demands a specific set of trained muscular responses; the leg and foot movements required of the boxer, the hammer thrower and the high jumper are simply not compatible. Again, while both the 100 metre sprinter and the soccer forward have to be able to run and accelerate, with the forward the real burst of acceleration has to be over five yards, in order to gain advantage over the defender in a crowded penalty area, while the sprinter can accelerate more smoothly during the whole race.

The division of labour seems absolute, and in some ways has increased. It is unlikely that anyone will again emulate the achievements of Dennis Compton, who in the 1950s played soccer for Arsenal and cricket for Middlesex, and who was an international at both sports (and one of the outstanding cricketers of his generation). It is true that the cricketer Ian Botham did turn out for the lower division Scunthorpe United, but his achievements on the soccer field were limited. Certainly also within team sports there has been differentiation and specialisation, with specialist positions such as goalkeeper or wicketkeeper, pitcher or quarterback – and in American football there are even forwards used to playing in the offensive or defensive line.

However, apart from the single-player specialties such as pitcher, specialisation within team sports seems to be on the wane. Coaches of contemporary team sports increasingly ask that their top performers are able to play in any position on the outfield. The rise of one-day cricket has meant that almost everyone in the side must be able to bat and bowl adequately, and also to catch well and to move rapidly in the field and throw accurately over long distances. There is a constant search for the cricketing 'all-rounder' in that more limited sense (a search, for a new Botham, which has been one of the most debilitating factors in recent English cricket). Similarly, soccer players in most professional leagues (not yet, unfortunately, the English or Scottish) are no longer typecast as (skilful) forwards and (aggressive) defenders, but have to be able to play as creatively in defence as in attack, and defenders have to know how to exploit the gaps left in the field when their forwards are being closely marked.

Perhaps most remarkably, one modern phenomenon both in rugby and American football is what could be called the 'fast forward'. The type of players who in the past merely exploited their bulk to block opponents and shield the ball, and saw no need for speed, can now accelerate from a standing start and catch opponents of slighter build (and in rugby, the obverse is true: rugby backs are increasingly physically heavy, and increasingly good at tackling; the paradigm of this trend is the astonishing New Zealander Jonah Lomu). Whether this is the result of diet, new training methods, sports psychology, the ingestion of large amounts of currently illegal chemicals, or all of the above, the results are undeniably impressive. In some ways the sporting body has become less specialised. All athletes now work with weights; all athletic bodies have become heavier in build. Sprinters, who only twenty years ago trained for whippet-like shape and muscularity to minimise weight resistance, are now in possession of heavy musculature for power in acceleration and short-term stamina in muscle use. So power has often displaced suppleness as the physical ideal. The 1992 Olympic 100 metres champion, Linford Christie, has claimed that his abdominal muscles are so rigid that he cannot bend and touch his toes. There is still a great deal of event-specific specialisation (no doubt Christie's work with weights has been rather different from that of the average weightlifter), and long distance runners have yet to embrace the power musculature, but there is clear convergence in many areas of athletic training activity.

4. Rationalisation

This is the centre of Guttmann's argument. He claims that modern societies have designed new sports, or redesigned existing ones, along rational lines, with both the rule-bound sports themselves and the preparation for them susceptible to rational organisation. Rationalisation is present at almost every level of sport. Archery, he argues, is a rationalised form of hunting, with a target which is always attainable, and the usual rules and bureaucratic interventions to create equality of opportunity among contestants. Training for sports is increasingly rationalised, seen as 'sports science', with sub-areas of diet, physiology and medicine, and psychology, contributing to the preparation of both athlete and coach (and incidentally providing a range of interesting sports-related activities for middle-class professional work).

The point is difficult to contest in general. Both sports, and the individuals and organisations who prepare for them, are indeed organised around rational goals. But this is only one, very abstract, way of looking at the phenomenon of contemporary sports. Two qualifications can be offered to the rationalisation argument. Firstly, as with the secularisation argument, no-one seems to have told the performers or the public. Even the most casual glance at athletes' biographies will reveal a group of people in whose lives non-rational beliefs and activities are relatively important. Many are profoundly superstitious. As well as those who pray before entering the field of play, there are people who indulge in repeated dressing room and mealtime rituals and other routines designed to propitiate Lady Luck. Waiting in the toilet, every week, until everyone else is already on the pitch, is not cool, calculating judgment. The behaviour of many fans matches that of the athletes in its attention to superstitious detail. Turning the lights out in a particular order before going to the stadium, wearing a particular set of socks for the duration of a cup run, and similar rituals are carried out in order to invoke fortune. Many aspects of sport may be rational; people aren't.

Secondly, it is quite simply the case that some sports are not susceptible to rational prediction. Scientific preparation for an event like a 200 metre sprint can be impressively detailed. The athlete must be prepared to run along an identified track, across which no-one else may run. The muscles must be prepared to deliver maximum power for about twenty seconds. The best prepared athlete will win the race. Even in this case, the variable of the weather conditions cannot be prepared for. But in the 800 metre race, there are no defined tracks. At this point, the tactical as well as muscular performances of the other athletes will have a bearing on the result, whatever the scientific training of the individuals. The modelling of events such as this falls outside the realms of conventional sports science. It is not a 'rational' impossibility, as chapter five will argue, but the more variables there are (such as weather, tactics, the opponents' skill in improvising situations) the more the possibility of predicting the outcomes of sporting events becomes a matter of probability rather than certainty. Favourites in sprints win most races; favourites in cup finals only win the majority.

5. *Bureaucratic organisation*

Here Guttmann's argument is at its strongest. The growth
of bureaucratic regulation is an inescapable facet of
contemporary sporting life. Committees and councils
decide on the rules and regulations, award medals at
contests, and coaching certificates after courses of
education which they also oversee. Bureaucracies define
the limits of their sports – determining the size and shape
of playing areas, the types of playing surface and
equipment which can be used, the hours of play, the
number of officials who must be present, and so on. All
this denies choice to participants, who before bureaucratisation could decide all of these issues on the spot
before the start of play, choosing the number of players
per side, the number of substitutes allowed, which players
are permitted to handle the ball, or whatever.

Because they are guardians of the rules, the bureaucracies also enforce discipline within their sports, imposing
penalties such as fines, suspension or bans for infringe-
ment. They administer or oversee drug tests, again
punishing the recalcitrant. And they liaise with each other,
interacting at local, national and international levels to
produce tour itineraries, pick international committees,
and send delegations to each others' events.

All of which seems harmless enough. But there is a
tendency for these bureacracies to be grossly unrepresentative. The basic models, the first of these regulatory
committees to be up and running, were the MCC
(Marylebone Cricket Club) and the Jockey Club. Both are
in origin, and indeed remain, gentlemen's clubs. The
Jockey Club was in charge of horse racing in the United
Kingdom until the fiasco of the start of the 1993 Grand
National (when an unrecalled false start led the most
prestigious race in the British calendar to be declared
void). After this the Jockey Club agreed to cede power to a
more professional organisation. The MCC ruled English
cricket from the eighteenth century, and was one of the
most powerful voices in world cricket until very recently; it
still has ambitions in that direction. It is all-male
(specifically exempt from equal opportunities legislation),
and virtually all its members are upper-middle-class.

Successful players are occasionally given honorary membership, but players are on the whole unrepresented save on the selection committees for touring parties. Close liaison is maintained with the equally conservative committees which run the county game. More ordinary supporters are not represented. Under pressure from modernisers and professional administrators, and representatives from former colonies who tend to be rightly suspicious of the remaining vestiges of imperialism and racism within an organisation which used to represent the imperial rulers, and was at best ambivalent about apartheid South Africa, the power of the MCC is on the wane, though the right to wear its garish tie remains one of the most sought-after signs of social success within English society.

Sporting bureaucracies have inherited a very club-like distrust of democracy. Gentlemen's clubs early on worked out an almost fool-proof way of ensuring that only 'the right people' were let in the front door. People were proposed for membership by existing members, one of whom then had to second the proposal. If committee members did not approve of the nomination, they could exclude the proposed member through voting. Policing their own membership is a common tendency within the bureaucracies which control sport. Their members tend to be grossly unrepresentative of those whose sports they administer; dominated by the white male middle class, they are unlikely to have much representation for contemporary performers or crucial officials such as referees, and extremely unlikely to represent fans and their interests.

Finally it should be noted that this internally regulated bureaucratisation does not, again, sit easily with objectivity and equity in administrative decision-making. These bodies do police their sports; and like all such organisations they are open to corruption. In recent years a series of allegations have been made against what is arguably the most important committee in world sport, the International Olympic Committee itself. In their book *The Lords of the Rings*, the journalists Vyv Sympson and Andrew Jennings have claimed that there is a widespread abuse of this power.[27] Drug use is connived at, committee members are drowned in perks, and sponsorship and television deals are often an opportunity for speculation. Bureaucratisation without democratic representation is dangerous and not in the interests of performers or public.

6. *Quantification*　7. *The Quest for Records*

These really have to be dealt with together. As Guttmann says, quantification is an inescapable companion of modern sport. The stop-watch was invented in 1730, specifically in order to time races. Predictably, Guttmann maintains that the statistical breakdown of sporting achievement is simply an aspect of the system of gathering and analysing information which produces most political policy. There are unquestionably mountains of sporting statistical data. Much of this information is produced and kept by officials, and records are an important part of the official narrative of most sports and games; but for almost all sports there are also enthusiastic amateurs who collect and collate information and then correspond with other statisticians in order to verify it. Societies exist solely in order to compare this type of information. The object of such societies is usually to establish 'the truth' of sport, in so far as it can be reduced to the statistics of, for example, penalty points conceded, players sent off, the number of venues where a sport has been played, the dates of birth and death of athletes, and so on *ad infinitum*. Cricket and baseball are particularly prone to the investigations of these amateur statisticians, who often pursue their official counterparts through any means necessary until their version of events is accepted into the public record. The public record remains important in the presentation of sport; the statistics form a resumé of *public memory*, a condensed memory from which the realities of sport can be reconstructed. Newspapers, magazines and annual yearbooks are assiduous in their presentation of statistical information. If they are not, the amateur statisticians queue up to put them right.

The pursuit of records 'for their own sake' is an aspect of this demand for the statistical, and among participant athletes it no doubt feeds the fantasy desire for success, for what Guttmann calls 'a uniquely modern form of immortality'.[28] But this is a compromised appetite, a tributary of another modern desire. In most sports, but particularly in athletics, the pursuit of records involves the pursuit of careers or sponsorship. A few hundredths of a second can mean the difference between a long professional career replete with reward and the promise of a post-retirement life of ease, or a return to obscurity. So in many track and field events the irreducible absolutes of performance – victory in the shortest time possible, or with the longest or highest jump – are indeed the zenith of ambition. This was not always the case. As Guttmann claims, the Greeks were not interested about times, they just cared who won – and *only* who won. In some sports this is still the baseline position. Soccer in Europe, for example, is comparatively free from the plethora of statistics which compromises the coverage of American football. There are soccer statistics, of course – leading goalscorers are given awards, and teams with poor disciplinary records may be fined. But the only really important statistics in soccer are the simple tallies of victory, defeat, and trophies won. Yet there are real debates in soccer circles about whether even this basic information is useful, or whether it is the quality of victory (or even of play in defeat) which counts. Likewise in most team sports. The rebellion in 1993 of MCC members, outraged when David Gower, the most aesthetically gifted batsman in England, was not chosen to tour India (outrage which increased when the England team was subsequently beaten in all three Test matches, its heaviest defeat on the subcontinent and a 'brownwash' to match the earlier 'blackwashes' administered by West Indies), indicates that even in cricket, one of the most statisticophile of sports, the question of quality looms at least as large as that of quantity.

Sporting Hegemony

So Guttmann's positions must be qualified in some important ways; some would argue that the limits of the Weberian argument make it unsuitable as a basic position. Like the theories of Norbert Elias and his school, this is a theory of modernisation; in Guttmann's capable hands Weber's ideas about social changes become a theory of progress. There are other ways of viewing rationalisation and bureaucratisation. One of the more impressive sociological overviews of sport published in recent years is John Hargreaves's *Sport, Power and Culture*.[29] This book uses that theoretical warhorse of the British left in the 1980s, Gramsci's notion of 'hegemony', to argue that sport is one of the ways in which a dominant group in society exercises power, not through physical dominance, or even through the imposition of a dominant ideology, but through negotiation. Things may, in this model, get better, not smoothly or routinely, but after contestation and negotiation. Sport is here a battleground over which groups with conflicting interests contend for power.

According to most interpretative users of 'hegemony', power is gained and maintained through consent to the ruling ideas of the time; this consent is made by constant renegotiation. In the case of sport in Britain, then, groups of people are not coerced into it, but won over to it. In the mid-nineteenth century, some traditional sports were suppressed, but the newly routinised team sports were offered in their place, alongside major concessions: by the end of the nineteenth century it was common for Saturday to be a half-holiday, so that they could be played and watched. Again, despite resistance from middle-class amateurs, professionalism rapidly became the norm in soccer and rugby league, and very unofficially in Welsh rugby union. The sports had been reworked in the interests of the skilled working class, who provided most of the audience, and nearly all of the players, for the professional games. Soccer and rugby (and horse racing) were massively reported in the press; a whole popular literary culture quickly evolved to support the new enthusiasm.

Since the 1950s, Hargreaves claims, a rather similar process has occurred in which many people have gained from sporting provision. There are now far more participants in all sports; the national Sports Council, and local councils, support a vast variety of participant sports including angling, golf, and leisure sports like aerobics and swimming, as well as athletics and team games.

Hargreaves argues convincingly that while aspects of this provision may, as some old-fashioned Marxist accounts claim, have the effect of reproducing labour power, others do not. People can gain, in other words, without the state getting anything direct in return. Soccer may improve team discipline, which may then be transferred back to the factory floor; aerobics may make women fitter for both work and motherhood; fishing and snooker, however, will do neither. Finally, Hargreaves points out that the current relationships between sport, consumer culture and the electronic media are another accommodation, another form of negotiated hegemony. If sport is one of the central aspects of a consumer regime which aims to combine health and fitness, diet and nutrition and fashion in order to produce healthier, more 'youthful' and more sexually attractive people, well fair enough – except that this is a 'hegemony' which will exclude the old, the poor, and the unemployed.

Sport and the Politics of the Working Class

Hargreaves's interpretation is not the only one which we should set against the Weberian model offered by Guttmann. The set of values identifed by Guttmann makes 'sport' so much like 'work' that many commentators have identified the late Victorian sporting ethic with industrial capitalism: such comparisons are easy and in some ways convincing. Jean-Marie Brohm's work *Sport: A Prison of Measured Time* is an eloquent example of this type of argument.[30] Influenced by the political theorist Louis Althusser, Brohm sees sport as an aspect of the dominant ideology (discussed above in the introductory chapter). Association football provides a good example; it was the most popular late-Victorian team game and the first of the new team sports to become professionalised (in other words, players and managers are paid for their work). It is hardly surprising then, argues Brohm, that football reflects the order of industrial society, with the players, the workers, operating a strict division of labour (attack or offence; midfield; defence; goalkeeper) under their captain, whose role is like that of the foreman on the

industrial shop floor. The captain/foreman is responsible
to a manager, who in turn is accountable for the team
players' productivity to a board of directors. Success for
the team will usually mean higher profits for the directors
and shareholders. By far the majority of shareholders and
directors of football clubs were and are successful
businessmen. The players, on the other hand, were
treated contractually in the same way as factory
employees, with wages which were generous by working-
class standards, but with a maximum wage set low enough
to maintain their status as highly skilled workers and no
more. The very structure of the game, with its rational
goal, the team discipline needed to achieve it, and its
'prison of measured time', the ninety minute period of
play, reflects the practice of industrial labour.

Brohm's argument is convincing as far as it goes. But
notions of productivity and profit were not the only values
which operated within late-Victorian team sports. Both the
new sports, and the older established team game of cricket
(which was transformed from an opportunity for
gambling, with a circus of top players, paid by aristocrats,
touring the country and playing against each other or local
teams, into a set of representative contests between teams
representing towns or counties), were also overwritten by a
set of beliefs about honest 'fair play', and the importance
of participation rather than victory; and by a whole
complex of ideas of 'team spirit', in which disciplined
personal commitment led to the sacrifice of the individual
for the team, the school, and the nation. All these values
can be associated with the late-nineteenth century
Imperial bureaucracy; all remain utterly crucial ideas for
any organised sport, and the discourses of journalism and
sports science which surround them; they help to
construct the sporting body and its possibilities. These are
not, as Brohm takes for granted, simply the values of
capitalism; notions of team spirit and the sacrifice of the
self in its interest are in many ways more compatible with
trade unionism, or even socialism, than the individualism
which drives capitalist accumulation – as the importance
given to sporting performance by the former Communist
countries of East Europe and the Soviet Union shows.

The so-called Eastern Bloc countries tried to demonstrate the superiority of their political system through success at international sport: perhaps the highlight from their point of view being the defeat by the USSR of the USA basketball team in the 1982 Olympic Games – the only defeat so far suffered by the (fully professional) American basketball team at the Olympics. However, team sport is not necessarily all about nation, or political ideology, and it is not simply a reflection of an existing economic order. Even the sporting successes of socialist countries were not only about socialism, but were also driven by the profound rivalries of national ideology which will be found within any imperial system: the intense and violent ice hockey match played at the 1968 Winter Olympics between the Soviet Union and Czechoslovakia, which had just been invaded by troops from other Communist countries seeking to save it from democracy, was not a celebration of socialist fraternity, but warfare by other means, just as the East-West confrontations were. Even in East Europe, sport was dominated by narratives of nation.

Notes

1. A good account is M.I. Finley and H.W. Pleket, *The Olympic Games*, Penguin, Harmondsworth 1976.

2. A. Blue, *Grace Under Pressure: The Emergence of Women in Sport*, Sidgwick & Jackson, London 1987, p93.

3. The Bakhtininian basics will be found in M. Bakhtin, *Rabelais and his World*, trans. H. Isialsky, M.I.T. Press, Cambridge, Massachusetts 1981. For an application of Bakhtin's ideas to the world of the sporting crowd, see M. Hoy, 'Joyful Mayhem: Bakhtin, Football Songs and the Carnivalesque', *Text and Performance Quarterly*, Number 14, October 1994, pp1-17.

4. E.G. Robert Darnton, *The Great Cat Massacre and Other Episodes in French Cultural History*, London, Allen Lane 1984.

5. P. Stallybrass and A. White, *The Politics and Poetics of Transgression*, Methuen, London 1986.

6. R. Sennett, *The Fall of Public Man*, Faber, London 1986.

7. Key texts of this set of arguments are N. Elias, *The Civilising Process: The History of Manners*, Blackwell, Oxford, 1978; Elias, *The Civilising Process: State Formation and Civilisation*, Blackwell, Oxford 1982; Elias and E. Dunning, *The Quest for Excitement: Sport and Leisure in the Civilising Process*, Blackwell, Oxford 1986; Dunning and C. Rojak (eds), *Sport and Leisure in the Civilising Process*, Routledge, London 1992.

8. Jennifer Hargreaves, *op.cit.*, p16.

9. S. Cohen, *Folk Devils and Moral Panics*, Hamish Hamilton, London 1971.

10. See John Hargreaves, *Sport, Power and Culture*, Polity Press, Cambridge 1986, pp91-2.

11. B. Houlihan, *The Government and Politics of Sport*, Routledge, London 1991, pp25.

12. W. Vamplew, *Pay Up and Play the Game: Professional Sport in Britain 1875-1914*, Cambridge University Press, Cambridge 1988.

13. See *The Independent*, December 7, 8, 1994.

14. E. Showalter, *The Female Malady: Women, Madness and English Culture 1830-1980*, Virago, London 1987, Chapter 7.

15. H. Wilkinson, *Genderquake*, Demos, London 1994; see also G. Mulgan and H. Wilkinson, *Freedom's Children*, Demos, London 1995.

16. See Bourdieu, 'How Can One Be a Sports Fan', p355.

17. A good account of the historical struggles over game is P.B. Munsche, *Gentlemen and Poachers: The English Game Laws* 1671-1831, Cambridge University Press, Cambridge 1981; see also E.P. Thompson, *Whigs and Hunters*, Penguin, Harmondsworth 1978.

18. G. Deghy, *Noble and Manly: The Story of the National Sporting Club*, Hutchinson, London 1956.

19. The key text is A. Guttmann, *From Ritual to Record*.

20. Guttmann, *ibid.*, p26.

21. G. Jarvie and J. Maguire, *Sport and Leisure in Social Thought*, Routledge, London 1994, p118.

22. Jennifer Hargreaves, *op.cit.*, p232.

23. Quoted in J.F. Coghlan and I.M. Webb, *Sport and British Politics Since 1960*, Falmer Press, Brighton 1990, p109.

24. P. McIntosh, 'The Olympic Games', *Citius Altius Fortius*, The Design Museum, February 1990, p17.

25. D. Sutherland, *The Mad Hatters Great Sporting Eccentrics of the Nineteenth Century*, Robert Hale, London 1987, p46.

26. R. Cashman, *Patrons, Players and the Crowd: The Phenomenon of Indian Cricket*, Orient Longman, New Delhi 1980, pp26-28.

27. V. Sympson and A. Jennings, *The Lords of the Rings: Power, Money and Drugs in the Modern Olympics*, Simon and Schuster, London 1992.

28. Guttmann, *op.cit.*, p55.

29. John Hargreaves, *op.cit.* My thanks to Sally Alexander for bringing this book to my attention.

30. J-M. Brohm, *Sport: A Prison of Measured Time* trans. I. Fraser, Ink Links, 1978. Note the defensive preface about intellectuals and sport; compare the approach of B. Rigauer, in *Sport and Work*, trans. A. Guttmann, New York 1981; and see the commentary offered in Guttmann, chapter. 2, 'Capitalism, Protestantism and Modern Sport'.

3 The Sporting Nation – and After?

How is it possible for sport to assume the mantle of national representation so easily? Since the re-creation of sport in industrial Britain, it has had this role. Wherever and in whatever ways sport is now used, in its emergent form in late nineteenth century Britain it was above all about *place*: place of work, or of education, or locality, or nation. Sport has always, therefore, made some contribution to a sense of community, whether imagined or experienced. Organised team sport began in the 1860s with teams chosen to represent schools, universities and, within a few years, nations; within twenty years teams of working-class men were being chosen, and paid, to represent towns and districts. Here the sense of place was that of the organisers of the team, and above all of local spectators, rather than of the participants. Again we must stress that it is in the imagination, the fantasy, of the spectators that the events on the field of play are allowed to assume the mantle of representation: sport helped the community to imagine itself. It did not matter to the local supporters that North London football club Tottenham Hotspur's FA Cup winning team of 1901 contained players from Wales, Scotland and the north of England, but not a single North Londoner. In the same way, more recently, it did not matter to members of Oxford University that the majority of the people in the crews who won thirteen consecutive Boat Races in the 1970s and 1980s were American postgraduates, virtually professional athletes in full-time training, rather than the amateur

British undergraduates who had pioneered the contest in the nineteenth century.

The Americans were eager to represent Oxford (and Cambridge, which quickly followed the Oxford example, and even won a few races in the early 1990s), partly because during the late nineteenth century the contradictory sporting ideals, and many of the games that went with them, were exported worldwide as an aspect of British imperialism; however, the American postgraduate rower is more like a professional than his British counterpart because of the different growth of sport inside the American educational system. The American universities, always more democratic than the British, and therefore more important to American cultural and commercial life as a whole, had evolved many of their own sporting traditions in parallel with the British. Although many of the ideals of the healthy body, the training of an elite, and fair play were accepted on both sides of the pond, American students were quick to play their own version of football, and by the end of the century the universities were providing many of the players for the professional football leagues: a very similar game, and professional leagues, evolved at the same time in the universities of Canada. English universities also provided cricketers and rugby internationals – but most of these played, even at the highest level, as amateurs. The class-based gap between amateur and professional sport was never quite the same in America as Britain, for all the snobbishness of the Ivy League universities of Harvard, Yale and Princeton. During the twentieth century the American college circuit has also become the crucial feeder for professional basketball, baseball and athletics.

Nation and the International Festival

Given the dominance of professionalism in the team games played and followed throughout the world, it is surprising perhaps that the most important international festival of sport, the Olympic Games, remains (in name at least) amateur, and that the most important Olympic sport, athletics, is controlled by an organisation which calls itself the International Amateur Athletic Federation. The Games were revived at the end of the nineteenth century by a French aristocrat, Baron Pierre de Coubertin, who had imbibed the British beliefs about fair play and the nobility of the amateur contest along with his classical education, and who turned to the example of the classical Greek sporting festival as a means of bringing peaceful competition to the world. De Coubertin was interpreting the ancient games (which through most of their thousand years were in fact fully professional, and which did not, as he thought, prevent warfare) through the matrix of his own cultural concerns – as we all do. He was convinced that the version of competitive sport he had encountered in the British public schools was the best. Other emerging national sporting traditions, which in Germany and Scandinavia included forms of gymnastics which emphasised health, fitness and the beauty of movement rather than competition, were ignored in favour of the British model. Even the Olympic motto is not about beauty, health or efficiency but strength and competition: 'Citius, Fortius, Altius' (better, stronger, higher).

The Scandinavian tradition was also open to female participation, but the Baron's vision, again influenced by the single-sex British public schools he had visited, was an exclusively masculine one; he was a life-long opponent of the participation of women in 'his' games. So while De Coubertin ignored aspects of the ancient games such as their professionalism and their routine violence (death in wrestling, and in another fighting event, the Pankration, was not uncommon) he insisted on holding to original practice when it suited him, as in the absence of female participation at the original Olympic meetings. 'Women', he remarked, 'have but one task, that of covering the winner with garlands'.[1] In one other respect he tried to reproduce the ancient Greek games, which were restricted to members of the ruling groups of their societies: he assumed that his games were to be part of the training of an elite. The public schools, which had played a part in the transformation of sport towards the regulatory model identified by Guttmann, also assumed that the training sport gave in teamwork, leadership, and the ability to implement strategy would be important to the future ruling elites – though they also spread their games down the social scale through churches and associated city mission schemes. Most of the early competitors in the Olympic Games, however, were indeed young people from the ruling elites of their countries: people who could afford to be amateur. (A rival quadrennial festival, the Workers' Games, which was also for amateurs but which de-emphasised the competitive element, was popular in the inter-war period, but effectively ended when the Barcelona Workers' Games of 1936 was interrupted by the Spanish Civil War).

Even amateur contests needed money for publicity, travel and accommodation, the construction of stadia, and so forth. Partly because of this, and much to De Coubertin's dismay, the amateur tendency among participants was almost immediately compromised by commercialism among those staging the events. The first three modern Olympiads were held in cities with concurrent trade exhibitions, and in Paris in 1904 in particular, the athletic competitions were seen to be less important than the trader's displays. Reacting against this snub to his amateur ideal, De Coubertin then organised another, commerce-free games at Olympia itself in 1906; but though the process of commercialisation was slowed until recently, the identification of the Games with commercial opportunities for the world's major cities could not be completely undone. Montreal in 1978 was the last Olympic meeting to make a loss for its host city. Since then, profits from the staging have been enormous. Nowadays, the competition among cities for the right to stage the Games is as fierce as any of the contests on track or field, and the buying and selling of the Games has become the most important function for the International Olympic Committee.

Several further factors have tended to undermine the spirit of amateur and open competition in which De Coubertin believed: as well as the continuous presence of commercialism, there is the regimentation of athletes into national teams (participants had to be members of a national team, picked by the relevant national Olympic Committee, from 1912). This system of representation was itself a prominent part of the Greek legacy, and of the development of the British games ethic. The 'nationalisation' of the Games has led to the politicisation of athletics;

the Games became a prominent part of the politics of the Cold War in a way which would have been impossible if they had been events open simply to those clocking the best times in particular events. Similarly, the politics of race have been played out through the Olympics at the level of the nation state. The abuse of the Olympic ideal in the name of racial beliefs was clearly evident at the Berlin Olympics of 1936. But the movement remains astonishingly successful. Despite Berlin, the Games survived World War Two, and despite the increasing professionalism of the organisation of athletes in communist countries, the cult of the amateur athlete remained powerful until the 1960s.

At this point it became clear that athletes were pawns in other games. The continuous, and potentially dangerous, taint of nationalism had been joined by the playing out on the world sports stage of rival ideologies: particular examples were the banning of South Africa from international competition over the policy of apartheid (and subsequent boycotts directed against nations which competed against South Africa at non-Olympic sports, such as New Zealand over rugby), the massacre of Israeli athletes by Palestinians at the Munich Olympics in 1972, and the demonstrations in favour of Black Power by successful American athletes at Mexico in 1968. More generally, even in the comments of the least politically sensitive sports journalists, it was clear that the Cold War was being fought on the Olympic playing fields as surely as it was in Vietnam and Afghanistan. Boycotts of the Games in Los Angeles (by East Europeans) and Moscow (by some western states) were aspects of this battle. But there was a direct contest on the playing fields themselves, a contest which, proportionately at least, was won by a communist state, East Germany. Though strictly speaking more medals per head of the population have been won by the Scandinavian countries (Finland, Norway, Sweden and Denmark), so many medals were won by East Germans, and stridently claimed by them as victories for socialism, that their methods began to receive critical, indeed hostile, worldwide attention. So, more recently, have the methods adopted by coaches of the female middle-distance runners from China who have broken records at will in the last few years, to the sceptical disapproval of those who assume their claimed special diets to be enriched by illegal chemicals, as was routinely the case in East Germany.

The East German state virtually forced any able child to train full-time as an athlete; young male and female athletes (and other sportspeople) were identified as potiential stars of the future through a series of biological and psychological tests, and were given designated jobs as soon as they were old enough for them, to preserve their 'amateur' status – but they remained in permanent training. The East German state invested a great deal of money in technical facilities and ensured that its coaches were well-trained and qualified. These methods were especially effective in procuring success for women, partly because the competition was weaker. Women in the West, constrained by dominant notions of femininity, were unwilling to train for strength and muscle bulk; East European women were willing to work for both (or perhaps were not given the choice), and thereby won more medals. West Europeans, Americans and others responded to this 'shamateurism' by seeking collegiate or commercial sponsors to pay their 'expenses': which again meant that many of them became full-time professionals in all but name. Those who could not attain such sponsorship, and people from the 'Third World' whose governments could not afford adequate training facilities, were at a very severe disadvantage.

Another expensive form of unfair advantage was the use of medical and chemical techniques to improve performance. During and after the 1960s, athletes from both 'sides' of the Cold War increasingly turned to drugs to control nervousness, to increase muscle bulk or stamina, or (in female gymnasts) to delay the onset of puberty. This has always been, as it remains, a difficult and divisive issue. The various national and international sporting authorities have reluctantly considered the problem, as it clearly denies De Coubertin's amateur ideal of free competition without unfair advantage. They agree in principle to the banning of all drugs which could give one athlete an advantage over another; yet there are many documented cases of national officials conniving in their athlete's drugtaking: one issue current at the time of writing was that of German athlete Katrin Krabbe, whose coaches as well as German national officials and journalists seemed ambivalent about the banning of a potential world-beater. Another was that of the British middle-distance runner Diane Modahl, whose appeal against a positive test which had shown massive (potentially fatal) amounts of testosterone was turned down after a great deal of internal debate about the consequences for Britain's place in the athletics world if her appeal should be upheld. Meanwhile there was a campaign in the British tabloid press, questioning the probity of the Portuguese laboratory which had carried out the tests on Modahl, who eventually won a second appeal on precisely the grounds that the laboratory had not stored its samples properly.

Drugtaking is viewed ambivalently by those who wish for success, and amateurism is also supported verbally more than by sanction. The recent introduction of an Olympic tennis contest in which young members of the professional tennis circus compete is one strong signal that the Olympics will soon become another circus itself rather than the festival of competing nationalities and ideologies we have become used to since World War Two. Paradoxically, it has been the rusting of the Iron Curtain which has spelt the final end of amateurism. Now that there are no Eastern Bloc countries left to pay lip service to an ideal which they had in fact systematically abused, pressures for a fully, openly professional athletic circuit which includes the Olympic festivals may well become irresistible. One alternative model, already being con- sidered by the International Olympic Committee, would devalue the Olympics into a competition for the under-23s, which would remain a nominally amateur contest, but the winners here would then become fully professional and join the world athletic circus, with the highlight of this circus being the biennial world athletic championships.

These problems – of cheating by drugs or shamateu- rism, the intense political debates and activities and so on – are a sign of the importance of the Games. The success of the Olympics has provided one model for all other sports played worldwide: the international championship held every four years. The gap is long enough to give opportunities for a new generation of young performers to compete at the highest level, and long enough for new sponsors and advertisers to be attracted to these festivals without much fear of overkill; but short enough for its role in the marking of time, and the ritual construction of nationality and stardom, to be effective. There are Olympic-style Student Games, Asian Games, Pan-American, African, and Commonwealth Games, Gay and Lesbian Games, and Games for disabled people, all of which use the Olympic model of four-year festivals.

The football 'world cup' was the first single-sport festival to follow the Olympics and institute a quadrennial championship designed around contests between teams of national representatives; it has since been joined by two of the other British exports, cricket and rugby union (and at a lower level of publicity by many other team sports such as rugby league, hockey and lacrosse). The soccer world cup is truly international, with teams from every nation in the world entering the competition and first competing, during the intervening three years, in a qualifying competition, for a place in the final series. In cricket and rugby the number of nations competing is smaller, and largely confined to the countries with which Britain had a direct colonial relationship (for example, cricket in Sri Lanka) or a commanding economic relationship (for example, rugby in Argentina), though this is not a universal prescription. Holland and Denmark are cricketing nations – a few Dutch and Danish players play professional county cricket in England, and teams representing each nation play in the play-off competition for the cricket world cup. Holland and Denmark were also represented in the women's cricket world cup held in Britain in 1993. In the case of the soccer world cup, an international festival has gradually been turned into a marketing opportunity, surrounded by the apparatus of sponsorship; in the more recent cricket and rugby union world cups, it was always part of the strategy for these festivals to 'modernise' the games (as the organisers saw it) and launch them as platforms for players, sponsors and officials alike to profit. The idea of nation, which has been associated with these team sports for over a century, is still at present a powerful aspect of this modernisation;

whether it will remain so is a point chapter five will discuss.

The relationship between these international festivals, modernisation and commercialisation is an assumption which can only at present be applied to men's sport. Rugby union, until 1995 one of the last notionally amateur men's team sports, has now lost this status, partly because of the commercial success of its world cup. It is rapidly becoming a game with an elite of well-rewarded players and a hinterland of semi-professionals and amateurs. Women's cricket and lacrosse, both of which held world cup competitions in 1993, have been celebrations far more in the spirit of the amateur tradition, with few sponsors (and many, if not all, of the players actually paying their own way). These women's team game championships are, then, élitist in the rather different sense that not everyone can afford the time off work, education or other activities to play them.

Festival and Place

Other international festival events, the various open tennis and golf championships, the city marathons and so on, are held on an annual basis. Even here, though in open competitions (which are 'open' to anyone qualified to enter, rather than people of one nationality or locality, or the members of the club hosting the contest) the sense of place is less clearly reinforced by nation, nationalism is still a powerful means of interpreting the events. The city marathons and half-marathons, for instance, offer one of the very few opportunities for local people to celebrate their own spaces through amateur sport but with the national attention of the media. Paradoxically (and perhaps unfortunately), however, they run alongside a circus of professional distance runners for whom the abstract distance, rather than any particular space, is the goal – together with prize and appearance money, and disproportionate media attention.

'Open' tennis and golf championships, though no longer open in the senses of mixing amateurs and professionals, or the members of local clubs with visiting players, are a chance for local people and national

television audiences to see the world's best at any
particular sport. They are gladiatorial circus events. Yet it
is often considered important, especially by the national
media, that, for example, no British player has won the
singles competition at the London tennis championship,
Wimbledon, since Virginia Wade's victory in 1977; similar
national concern was expressed in the USA when
European players won the United States Open Golf
championship three times in a row, and the European
team then won the Ryder Cup twice in successive years, at
the end of the 1980s. At a time of sensed national decline –
for example, the early 1990s, with economic recession and
very high unemployment – the burden placed by the
media on 'their' national sporting figures can seem heavy,
especially if they too fail in international competition. In
early 1993 opinion polls reported that the only person in
England held in lower esteem than Prime Minister John
Major was the manager of the England football team,
Graham Taylor. As I remarked above when discussing the
figure of the star/scapegoat, such perceived failures are
often in effect excommunicated by those who have
supported them, and in Graham Taylor's case this was
done quite dramatically. Taylor's failure to lead his team
to the 1994 World Cup finals was marked with a riveting
television documentary which was edited so as to imply
that his knowledge of the game and his coaching abilities
were as limited as his vocabulary.

But is all this really important? These public burdens,
the continuous and heated debate which surrounds
national performance in sport, can seem ridiculous to
those for whom sport is no more than '11 men running
after a ball', or some similar formula expressing
bewildered contempt. This unfortunate view is still
popular in some intellectual circles. It is one of the reasons
for the continuing lack of attention given to sport by
academia (the myth of academics as grown-up school
swots, incapable of running, jumping or kicking a ball, still
has a lot going for it), which in turn helps to obscure the
meanings of sport, even the crucial relation between sport
and nation. Thanks to the emergence of sport via imperial
relations and international competitions such as the
Olympics, the relationship between sport and nationalism

remains the most important way through which both sport and nation are constructed, performed, and seen, and no understanding of contemporary sport can emerge without teasing out some of the basic issues in the problem.

The Technology of Modern Sport

As I pointed out above, sport in the modern sense emerged first in Britain, in the generations after industrialisation and the coming to parliamentary power of the industrial middle class. This is not just so in the sense of *A Prison of Measured Time*. From the start of this process, technological change accompanied the games and the belief systems they were played within. Industrial power itself, in particular the building of the railways, was vital in turning sport from a local to a national, and potentially international, event. Previous sporting competitions had played their part in the construction of local identities, both reinforcing and cutting across the existing divisions of class: but the only truly national rituals were military and monarchic – the celebrations of victories or coronations. All sports, including those already well established, were changed as technological developments compressed space and time.

National competition in horse racing, for example, was virtually impossible before rail transport enabled the animals to travel long distances (before this they had to walk to meetings – even walking could tire them so as to be uncompetitive, so an upper limit of thirty miles was accepted for race meetings; they were, therefore, all local). From the middle of the nineteenth century, thanks to trains, horse racing developed first a national and then an international dimension. Horses could be carried long distances without becoming tired, and an eager public could more easily travel the country to watch them, while the development of communication technologies, including national and local newspapers, the telegraph and the telephone, helped the gambling side of the industry. Some racecourses were constructed by the side of railway tracks, as at Sandown Park in Surrey. Soon a circuit of meetings of national importance developed, involving meetings at

York and Liverpool as well as those close to London like Sandown, Ascot and Epsom. These meetings were as important socially as they were as sporting occasions: attended by the local gentry and businessmen, and many from the ruling élite in London, they formed an important site for the meeting of local and national interests. Technology and capital, operating on sport, had produced a new set of social and spatial relationships.

Fox-hunting was likewise transformed by the railway from a series of local packs to a national sporting and social circuit; London residents like the novelist Anthony Trollope and the journalist Walter Bagehot would travel by train to meetings in the Midlands or the West Country, often sending their favourite horses ahead of them. Through this transformation, fox-hunting became more important as a national pastime; a small scale local event, hardly present in art and literature in the early eighteenth century, was transformed during the nineteenth century into a national symbol celebrated in endless sporting prints and in the writings of many middle-class and aristocratic writers like Nimrod, Surtees and Trollope himself.[2] At the same time it became less important as a celebration of the local – it became a sport of the wealthy commuter rather than the local resident. The railways also opened up shooting and fishing estates to a metropolitan constituency, again allowing easier access to these pastimes to those who were wealthy, but not local, and not necessarily aristocratic. The shooting of game, and fishing, became seasonal country pursuits for the privileged city dweller; through the use of the related technology, the steam ship, the colonial 'big game hunt' became a routine sport for the wealthy, a form of ecocide practised with enthusiasm until in many cases stocks of game were on the point of extinction. Similarly in the twentieth century, thanks to the growth of air travel, field sports have become internationalised, with people travelling from all over the world to stalk and shoot deer in Scotland, for example.

Team sport, which developed in its organised form from the 1860s, was immediately a part of the railway age: it was easy for teams representing localities and nations to compete against each other (and by the use of steam ships, to begin regular international competition; cricket tours

involving teams from England, Australia, the United
States and Canada were routine by the end of the
nineteenth century; again, the development of long-haul
passenger flight has since made these and other sporting
circuses truly and permanently international). The first
football international (between England and Scotland)
took place in 1870. This fixture, played between teams of
former public school pupils, was played well before the
emergence of the first local league, the Football League in
1888, which began to pit teams of working-class men
representing industrial districts of the English north and
midlands against each other in an organised structure with
a prize, the league championship, at the end of the season.

The New Team Games and the Nation

Soccer did not evolve directly from the popular games
which had been played in the villages; the rules were
worked out at Cambridge University in the 1850s, as
young men from the varous public schools (each of which
had their own ball games) tried to set up a contest with
mutually agreed rules. But the memories and remaining
practices of the 'folk' game helped to spread the reformed
version, which was eagerly propagated by young Oxford
and Cambridge graduates as they worked in education,
industry and the church. The foundation of the Football
League, however, played a transforming role in the way in
which football as a team sport contributed to national
identities, by undermining the élitism of the public school
based Football Association. Within a generation the
Football League permitted professionalism. Professional
players soon achieved levels of fitness which led to the
virtual disappearance of the amateur from the international scene. The self-perpetuating oligarchy of public
school and university graduates chosen to represent
England by the committee of the Football Association
(which also consisted of public school and university
graduates) was replaced by another self-perpetuating
oligarchy of working-class professionals. However, the
players for the national team were still chosen by a
committee of the Football Association (a system which

disappeared only in 1963 with the appointment of the first full-time England team manager) but were picked, ostensibly at least, on merit rather than birth or education.

So at the end of the nineteenth century, when most working men had the vote, but before the emergence of the Labour Party into parliamentary politics, the nation was represented at this most popular sport by working-class men. It was therefore rather easier for the majority of the population to identify with this symbol of nationhood than with parliamentary politics. Through this forty-year process from the 1860s, a new form of national identity had been constructed, through aristocratic-middle-class interaction, and then, in this limited but important sense, democratised. Historian Richard Holt has argued that 'playing the game', in its different class versions, was internalised by people as an ideology of constitutionalism. In other words, as they accepted the rules of the various team sports, so they accepted the rules of the political game, and did not turn to the extreme left or right. Politicians and other members of the establishment were aware of this and signalled their acceptance of it by displaying enthusiasm for the democratic sports. In the early twentieth century, it became routine for monarchs and prime ministers to attend cup finals and test matches; similarly, US presidential candidates are always careful to acknowledge some allegiance to football and baseball teams as a sign of their reciprocal acceptance of this democratic, representative activity.

The links between this form of national identity and a more general patriotism were amply and tragically displayed during World War One, as (working-class) men were led from the trenches to their deaths by their (middle-class and aristocratic) junior officers, kicking footballs and rugby balls ahead of them as they advanced into enemy gunfire. Thus the classes were united in team spirit, in the body language of the great game – in what was routinely referred to as the ultimate sacrifice. The military origin of sport may be debatable; the use of team sport as a means of binding the troops into a common culture is not; one German commentator, Rudolf Kircher, suggested that British stamina in the trenches owed something to sport.[3] Sport remains an important part of military culture, with regimental and inter-service competitions evoking great pride and commitment in teams which again are picked on sporting ability, mixing junior officers and other ranks. The implied relationship between sport, team-work and command is perfectly summarised in Sir Henry Newbolt's poem *Vitai Lampada* (1912):

> There's a breathless hush in the Close tonight—
> Ten to make and the match to win—
> A bumping pitch and a blinding light,
> An hour to play and the last man in.
> And it's not for the sake of a ribboned coat,
> Or the selfish hope of a season's fame,
> But his captain's hand on his shoulder smote—
> 'Play up! play up! and play the game!'
>
> The sand of the desert is sodden red,—
> Red with the wreck of a square that broke;—
> The Gatling's jammed and the Colonel dead,
> And the regiment blind with dust and smoke.
> The river of death has brimmed his banks,
> And England's far, and Honour a name,
> But the voice of a schoolboy rallies the ranks:
> 'Play up! play up! and play the game!'
>
> This is the word that year by year,
> While in her place the School is set,
> Every one of her sons must hear,
> And none that hears it dare forget.
> This they all with a joyful mind
> Bear through life like a torch in flame,
> And falling fling to the host behind—
> 'Play up! play up! and play the game!'

Through this and hundreds of other poems and school songs and stories, the connection between school team spirit, nation, and the sacrifice of the individual life was made. A similar fictional construction allowed Raffles, the amateur cracksman, the cricket-playing hero of E.W. Hornung's stories, to atone for his guilt by dying on the field of battle. Hornung's character is a cricketer who plays as a gentleman amateur, but who can afford to do this not through independent income, but because he steals from the houses of his wealthy friends – to the annoyance of the true 'professional' criminals. The stories are throughout an interesting aspect of the debates about amateurism, gentlemanly status, and the place of sport in society. In the final story, set during the Boer War of 1899–1901, Raffles narrates his own death at the hand of his Boer sniper opponent as a cricketing contest between two bowlers. ' "Another over at the grey felt hat", said he; "by Jove, though, I believe he's having an over at me" '[4]; he goes on to thank the general for the privilege of his position in the front line – just before being shot and killed. In France, the 1914–18 war was welcomed in similar terms, one young Parisian remarking 'la guerre . . . c'est la sport pour le vrai' (war . . . it's sport for real), while the cycling magazine *L'Auto* wrote on the outbreak of war that 'This is the big match . . . and you must use every trick you've learned in sport'.[5]

This combination of sport, military discipline, and sacrifice was a powerful model through which the ruling élite saw both their own role and their relation to others, including their colonial subjects. One colony at least, the Sudan, was known as 'the land of blacks ruled by blues': virtually all the civil servants working in the Sudan had strong athletic records at school and university ('blue' was the official colour those who had represented the Universities of Oxford and Cambridge were permitted to wear).[6] British sports were made available to local peoples, and in some ways this form of cultural imperialism was a positive attempt to cross the cultural boundaries of language, religion and custom which divided ruler from ruled. But the consequences were not always positive. In India, the local populations were taught cricket, and enthusiastically took up the game; but the prejudices of the British administrators meant that teams and competitions were formed based around religious communities – Sikhs, Hindus, Muslims, Parsis and so on – in an aspect of the vision of India through which the British tried to divide and rule, and succeeded in dividing when they no longer ruled (through the creation of Pakistan and India, and later Bangladesh – a process which cost millions of lives in 1947, and has led to several wars thereafter).

The vestiges of the official relationship between sport and nation remain in public sports policy.[7] There has been a Cabinet Minister responsible for sport in Britain since 1962; but very little in the way of consistent policy. Since the end of empire, state policy, especially at the level of local government, has tried to spread the benefits of sport outside the élite, and the classroom, with the building of national and regional sports centres and a Sports Council to advise on the development of sport. The Sports Council has tried to help both high achievement and in the words of its own campaign, 'Sport for All', no doubt in the hope that state-encouraged activity would foster respect for the state. There are also, here, serious concerns for the health of the population, and concerns that a sedentary population will be less healthy than one which is active and exercises regularly. In this regard, it is unfortunate that in the early 1990s, as the Treasury sought cuts in order to allow for lower levels of taxation, the Sports Council moved away from its attempts to promote 'Sport for All', and towards a system of funding excellence and the training of those identified as potential stars of the future. This is the East European model, copied already with some success in many areas of sport in Australia.

While both policies could, therefore, in some sense be called 'democratic', neither model was or is a universal panacea for the divisions in British society. People are not simply 'hailed into position' through the operation of cultural forms, however 'democratised' or internationally successful through élitism they may be. Team sport was born into a society riven by class divisions which were not dissolved by the cross-class participation in team sports. To some extent, in fact, late-nineteenth century moves towards professionalism re-emphasised the class divisions which the spread of the association football code had questioned as the public school missionaries spread their version of the game through the schools, churches and workplaces of the working class. Historian Wray Vamplew's ironically titled study, *Pay Up and Play the Game*, provides an authoritative survey of these contradictions.

Middle-class schools still propagated a belief in amateurism; some turned to rugby union as a result of the professionalisation of soccer, though the most powerful and politically influential of the schools – Eton, Winchester and Westminster for example – did not, and continue to play soccer today, though Eton and Winchester also practise football-like games peculiar to themselves. Amateur football evolved in parallel with the professional game. It was played by both middle- and working-class players, and was still popular enough, even in the 1950s, for crowds of 100,000 to attend the FA Amateur Cup Final. (The increasing implausibility of the term 'amateur', however, led to the ending of this competition in 1974). Football in England remains riven by class distinction, principally at the level of performance: at the time of writing there are no FA Premier League players with a public school education. Middle-class boys with talent as footballers are not encouraged to enter a game which, though 'professional', and with the potential to earn fortunes for its practitioners, carries too high a risk of failure. In other parts of the world, the professional game is not played exclusively by the working class. Because of this difference, French internationals Michel Platini and Eric Cantona, and German international Franz Beckenbauer, are national figures in rather different senses than British footballers like Gary Lineker or Ian Wright: in Cantona's case, we might even use the term 'intellectual' for this highly strung student of art and philosophy.

The slightly different takeup of the game overseas should not blind us to the fact that association football was and remains the most successful British cultural export of all time; and that it was exported in the particular forms established in Britain – as a local and national icon played and watched by massive numbers of working-class men. The association of the sport with international competition, and therefore with nationalism, was also, always, a part of the exported product. Football is a national icon important enough for one football international to have been the starting point for a war, between Honduras and El Salvador in 1969.

Cricket, sometimes portrayed positively as a less aggressive game than soccer, has also been associated with international political crises: India and Pakistan, for much of their post-1948 history on the brink of war, for a long time avoided international cricketing confrontation lest the defeated power should seek to heal the sporting injury in battle. More recently this policy has been reversed; the two countries played a test series in 1988 which helped to defuse tensions between the two nations. Cricket has, however, directly caused at least one diplomatic crisis: in 1932–3, an aggressive performance by an English touring team in Australia led to the threat that Australia would withdraw from the Commonwealth. Unlike football, cricket did not spread quickly throughout the world in the late nineteenth century: indeed, in the USA, where the game was part of the legacy of British culture and had been played since the eighteenth century, it was replaced by a rather faster English summer game, baseball. Cricket remained, on the whole, associated with countries which were at one time part of the British Empire.

In India, for instance, cricket is one of the increasingly few aspects of Indian culture which binds the communities together.[8] Since the end of the British Empire, commune-based cricket has largely been replaced by locally-based competition in which members of all religious communities compete on the same sides. Indian international teams, likewise, have incorporated Hindus, Sikhs, Muslims, Christians and Parsis; the commentaries on the game on All-India Radio, and the television presentations of district, zone and test matches, are a continuing force for unity. This is not to say that their effect is uniform across the whole country. The playing of cricket in India has always been constrained by matters of class and power. Early patrons were the princes, who used the game as part of their strategy of integrated power-sharing with the British. More recent patrons are the banking and industrial concerns of the big cities, whose teams hire the best players. As a participant and observed sport, the colonial and power relationships offered within the game make it the site of hybrid identities through which categories of faith and nation can be questioned and transcended, built and rebuilt. However, Indian cricket remains an urban rather than a village game; the active players, including international players, are overwhelmingly middle-class (though it is worth remembering that in a country with such a large population the middle class is at least 80 million strong); but the listeners and viewers are from all ranks. When India play Pakistan, or England, the former colonial power, the nation is more united than at any other time; national holidays are declared when England is defeated in a Test series.

It is important to stress that British cricket is similarly contradictory: hybrid identities are no longer the exclusive property of the former-colonised, if they ever were. It remains riven by the class distinctions which pervade soccer; but they operate rather differently. In cricket, the 'first-class' game, which had replaced the gambling circus during the nineteenth century, was played by a mixture of working-class professionals and middle-class and aristocratic amateurs. Though the distinction was observed in details such as separate dressing-rooms on many grounds, financially it was often a paper one, with amateurs claiming more in expenses than the profession-als received in wages; it was abolished in 1963, at around the same time that footballers were released from the restriction of the maximum wage imposed by the cartel of club owners, and became to all intents and purposes freelance 'middle-class' professionals rather than working-class employees. However, while the background of footballers remains surprisingly uniform, that of cricketers still shows a mix of middle- and working-class backgrounds; international teams representing England at cricket, which have included players with Caribbean and Asian ancestry, and from all social classes, have arguably reflected the total makeup of British society rather more accurately than international sides chosen to play professional football for England, Scotland or Wales. The women's game, still amateur, is still basically white and middle-class.

The class, regional and national divisions within the other British football game, rugby, are different again.

The primary division is between codes: the rugby league, based in the north of England, is fully professional and almost all its players are working-class; rugby union was until 1995 notionally amateur, and in England at least was still until recently played within an amateur structure. Rugby Union clubs played a series of traditional fixtures, without an organised championship; many of the players are middle-class 'professionals' in the rather different sense that they have jobs as management consultants or doctors. Only in 1988 did English club rugby union take to a league structure, with competitive fixtures leading to promotion and relegation, a championship, and at least informally, a system of player transfers between clubs. Almost immediately the fortunes of the national side improved dramatically. In makeup the English national side is still dominated by former public schoolboys and university graduates, but their attitude to the game is now more 'professional' in the sense that they train more regularly. Players, therefore, increased pressure on the game's administrators (who are all from the social élite which propagated the amateur ideal) to end compulsory amateur status and to allow them to earn money from the game; this was officially done in 1995. It is often alleged that rugby players in France and the southern hemisphere (New Zealand, Australia, South Africa) had always been professionals in all but name. Rugby union in Wales was never dominated by middle-class players, and therefore emerged as one of the chief carriers of national values in the same way, and at the same time, as professional soccer in England and Scotland, and most of the rest of the world.[9] Rugby union has achieved a similar position in the south-west of France, in New Zealand, in Afrikaans-speaking white South Africa, and in Western Australia. In all three former colonies, as with Wales (and as with Indian or West Indian cricket) victory over the former colonising power is regarded as the apogee of success.

In Ireland, too, a rugby victory over the English is a special occasion. Irish rugby is virtually the only thing which unites the religious and political divisions of the country – players are chosen from both the North and the Republic, from both Protestant and Catholic faiths. Soccer is also important to both divisions (unfortunately in this case there are two national sides); yet one of the ways in which Irish Catholics reacted to the growth of the new team sports in England was to reject them as an aspect of cultural imperialism, and to recreate their own sporting traditions. A Gaelic Athletic Association, closely associated with Irish nationalism, promoted specifically Irish games, and Gaelic football and hurling have been played since the late nineteenth century in Irish communities all over the world – including Irish communities in England and Scotland – though by and large they have not spread beyond those communities.

Perhaps the most important anomaly in this story of imperialism and internationalism is the position of the United States of America, which was emerging as one of the chief commercial rivals of Britain at the end of the nineteenth century, precisely the time at which soccer was colonising most of the rest of the world. The USA became the leading economic and military power during the twentieth century, and continues to be so. As in Britain, team games have been important in all aspects of American society: the entry into these sports of successive waves of immigrant populations, and perhaps especially the post-war entry of black people at the top levels of performance, have been vital to the creation and recreation of a sense of 'American' identity. Yet the games favoured by the Americans, baseball, basketball, football and ice hockey, remain on the fringes of popularity elsewhere in the world. This is despite the best efforts of American capital and media, which realises the potential of a stake in the broadcasting of world sports – this is one reason for the otherwise bizarre decision to stage the 1994 soccer World Cup in the USA. Despite this isolation, Americans call the playoffs between leagues which end each season in baseball the World Series: in fact only teams from the US leagues enter. Similarly, in motor racing, the Americans have the Indy-car series, which again they call a World Series despite its location in the USA (currently only one Indy-car race is run outside the USA, in Australia). No American team enters for the European-led Grand Prix circuit, which is soccer's only rival as a global television money-spinner – instead, attempts have been made to promote Indy-cars outside the USA. Only in individual sports such as boxing, golf, tennis and athletics do Americans compete regularly against the represen- tatives of other nations, and only in boxing can they be said to dominate; so the national emotional investment in boxing, athletics, golf and tennis is consequently higher than it is elsewhere in the world. American paranoia even here is such that poor American performance at the 1992 Olympics at Barcelona led many Americans to suggest that American sport should become completely isolationist; that no more American teams should compete for international prizes. Recent attempts to promote Ameri- can football in Europe have proved as ineffective, despite massive investment, as attempts in the 1970s and 1980s to promote professional soccer in the United States.

Why should this be? Why should the world power which has dominated so effortlessly in other aspects of culture, such as film and popular music have failed to dominate in sport? Or, perhaps even more puzzlingly, why do Europeans take MacDonalds beefburgers and large Coca Colas to their ringside seats in soccer stadia and not ball parks? Is it just that the Americans play the 'wrong' games? Clearly not. Soccer is played everywhere, in hot, cool and cold climates, and by people of every ethnic origin. Baseball, on the other hand, is only played professionally in the Americas (including the USA's arch-enemy Cuba), the former colony the Philippines, and Japan. The simplest explanation for this anomaly is that American power and hegemony were never translated into imperial rule on the British scale; for all the interventions in Vietnam and Central America, and its reluctant part in the two world wars, much of American foreign policy, throughout the twentieth century, has been 'isolationist'. In one of the exceptions to this isolationism, Japan after 1945, which was under thorough if informal American rule for a decade (and still plays host to over 40,000 American service personnel), there remains the second most popular baseball league in the world. Even here, however, as Japan tries to enter the world political and cultural system as an equal participant for the first time since 1945, baseball is losing its popularity and a national professional soccer league has been set up, with a view to a successful national side and the hosting of the soccer world cup in Japan early in the twenty-first century.

The Irish and American experiences emphasise that it is difficult to offer British imperial diffusion as simply 'the model' for the takeup of sport into national cultures – it would be equally difficult to offer the ancient Greeks as the only model. But the sports and ideologies of sport produced by Greece, Rome and Britain have probably been the most influential in the formation of the current world network of sporting competition. As it has been presented here, for all the problems and exclusions of class and gender, there is an identifiable, smooth relationship between various forms of sporting activity and ideas of time and place. Many people derive some of their strongest ideas of nation from sporting events: through these events and their media representations they can imagine their national, as well as local, communities. Sport can provide a narrative of emergence, of national growth, or of opposition; it can narrate collective, national aesthetic styles. Sport can be the supreme narrator of time, space and place.

But in the late twentieth century, for all the increasing power of ideologies of nation in the remnants of the communist world, the smooth relationships proposed in this model have been disrupted, if not completely broken. The operation of the media on the public, and the operation of the public on the media; the different takeup of sport by men and women, and by different ethnic groups; the sometimes disruptive presence of bodies of obsessive fans; the increasingly, narcissistically, obsessively structured bodies of the athletes themselves; the growth of the international sports circus in which talented players of all nationalities travel the world and compete with and against each other; all these in some ways undercut the very notion of an imaginable, national community, and certainly question the possibility of representing it through sport. What do they, or can they, put in its place?

Notes

1. A. Blue, *op.cit.*, p66.
2. See A. Trollope (ed), *British Sports and Pastimes*, Virtue & Co., 1868. A typical Trollope hunting scene is in *Is He Popenjoy?* (1878; Oxford

University Press 1948), Chapter VIII, 'Pugsby Brook'. Richard Holt makes similar points about field sports in nineteenth-century France; Holt, *op.cit.*, Chapter 2, 'The Spread of Field Sports'.

3. Cited in T. Mason, *Sport in Britain*, Faber, London 1988, p96.

4. E.W. Hornung, *Raffles – The Amateur Cracksman*, Souvenir Press, London 1984, p314.

5. Holt, *op.cit.*, p195.

6. A. Kirk-Green, 'Imperial Administration and the Athletic Imperative: The Case of the District Officer in Africa', in W.J. Baker and J.A. Mangan (eds), *Sport in Africa: Essays in Social History*, Africana Publishing, 1987, p96.

7. See B. Houlihan, *The Government and Politics of Sport*, Routledge 1991; and the more parochial J.F. Coghlan and I.M. Webb, *Sport and British Politics since 1960*, Falmer Press, Brighton 1990.

8. See in general on this Cashman, *op.cit.*.

9. G. Williams, 'From Popular Culture to Public Cliché: Image and Identity in Wales 1890-1914', in J.A. Mangan (ed), *Pleasure, Profit and Proselytism: British Culture and Sport at Home and Abroad 1700-1914*, Frank Cass, London 1988.

4   Placing the Performer, Placing the Observer

So locality, nation and empire have been represented by team sports and to a lesser extent by the more gladiatorial, individualised contests like tennis and golf. They have been able to offer their narratives of time, place and loyalty through the interaction of bureaucracies and systems of regulation and ownership, represented through players and their presentation to the public. The public response to all this has been to create a series of imagined communities mapped on to the bodies of the competitors, which then become the imaginary spaces through which subsequent sporting events can occur as public spectacles. This analysis continues with a discussion of the nature of spectatorship: of the role of the crowd, and the larger group I here refer to as 'the public' – people who participate in sport principally through informal conversation and the media. The participants in any sport, in other words, are not just the players, teams, managers, coaches or other officials: the spectators of these contests, including implicitly and occasionally explicitly whole nations and the massive global publics created by broadcast media, are also participants.

Whether any or all of this is necessarily 'a good thing' is debatable. Success in sport may help a participant or spectator to form a local or national identity. It may help resistance to imperialism, as with Gaelic sports, or adherence to some of the ideas of the imperial rulers, as with the early history of cricket in India. It may help resistance to or acceptance of the ideals of consumer capitalism, or communism, or social democracy. But it incontrovertibly leads and has led to personal, communal and international violence. Cricket and soccer have already been seen as the companions of warfare. Crowd riots at chariot races in ancient Rome and modern cricket matches in West Indies and Pakistan point to the continuing problems of crowd identification with teams and places. The phenomenon of football hooliganism is often seen at its most extreme both at the local level (say, Milan versus Inter) and at the international (for example, Holland versus England), where in each case groups of virtually identical young working-class males confront each other and assert their territorial rights and masculinities. No doubt both groups have negotiated for themselves some form of collective identity. The victims of the Heysel stadium disaster of 1986 (in which fans were crushed trying to escape from other aggressive fans), and in a more mediated way also those of the Hillsborough disaster of 1989 (crushed against barriers which had been installed to control and segregate fans, because of previous crowd violence of the sort which had occurred at Heysel), are testimony to the dangers of this kind of identification – to those of us who do not like violence, at least. Sport is important in the creation of public identities; but in their assertions of difference, these effects are troubling.

Public Identities

The introductory chapter argued that sport is an inescapable part of the background noise of contemporary culture. To some extent, then, whether they like it or not, all contemporary citizens are members of the public addressed by sport. For the purposes of this analysis, those who are interested in sport will be subdivided into categories of intensity of interest. The 'public' here is differentiated from both the enthusiastic 'supporters' and the obsessive 'fans', who are dealt with in the following sections. Principally here by 'the public' I mean people who hear and think about sport (including those who think negatively about it), but whose interest in it, if any, is through reading, listening to and watching the media rather than through direct contact as participants or observers of professional competitive sport. This definition of the public does include people who participate in some forms of personal health-related sporting activity such as jogging, aerobics or gymnasium-based working out, but not those who play (at any level) competitive sports which are regularly the subject of public comment. The general public, then, is informed about sport rather than active within it.

This leaves a large number of people who for the purposes of this essay I shall call the supporters, and the smaller group of fans. I include under the heading 'supporters' many people who could also be called participants. Any public sport is triangular in structure. The apex is professional, or at least nationally broadcast and reported. The base is amateur, not usually reported, and involves many people at different levels of commitment and ability: most have a playing career in their twenties, and then become administrators or otherwise continue to play a part in their clubs, within a general commitment to the game as a whole. Local rugby players, for instance, will almost always be supporters of their sport at national level. All of these people I bring under the heading 'supporter'.

In order to analyse the public perception of sport, we must first confront the ways in which information about sport becomes public. The public view of sport is largely mediated through the media's presentation of performers and prominent coaches, whose personal, medical and sexual successes and failures are recounted in the same way as those of any other category of 'star'. It should be remembered that this personalisation is reliant on the public position of the sport, and not the other way round – for all that players who transgress accepted social rules may be charged with bringing their sport into disrepute. In creating and sometimes destroying stars, the media are providing both the champions and scapegoats which societies seem to need.

The role of the media is also crucial in determining ways in which sports are ranked; these orders are usually implicit with other hierarchies based on class, gender, ethnicity and place. Some sports, or divisions within sports, are seen as of national importance, some of regional, and some as local, and are reported as such by both local and national media. Through these divisions, as well as many other similar divisions of the local, regional and national (for example, taste in beer, availability of jobs, cost of housing, languages) the public is addressed, and therefore people are helped to think of themselves, as members of an imagined community, as members of localities, regions and nations served and represented by sports and their players as much as by any local and national political system. At the local level, they may also be addressed as potential or actual players themselves. Local leagues for town or village sports are reported in the local press, and occasionally in the national media. In England, the final of the annual village cricket competition is widely reported. It is held at Lord's cricket ground, the premier national stadium for the sport. Though the event directly represents only at most a few thousand local people, the idea of village cricket is an important component of nostalgic Englishness, so in this case the local event becomes an aspect of the national imagined community – an aspect, indeed, of 'heritage culture'. Most local sporting events, however, such as the vast numbers of golf rounds played all over the world every week, are not reported: controversial speeches at golf club dinners are as likely to make local news as, say, the defeat of the club professional by the ladies captain.

Through the media's presentation the sports themselves are ranked in a hierarchy of importance, with the national team games and especially international competition receiving pride of place, and some sports (and, in most parts of the world, team sports involving women) receiving comparatively little coverage. There are occasional changes in this hierarchy and its media presentation: two recent examples in Britain, the rise and comparative fall of snooker, and the rise and more or less total fall of darts, owe a lot to the particular aptitudes of television, for which both games provided easy, and comparatively cheap, viewing in the early 1980s. Each then suffered from overexposure to a simple game, though in the case of darts, advertisers felt that the sport was too downmarket (it attracted viewers who were unlikely to buy what was advertised), and so in the end it failed as a television product. The darts players and their agents, having realised this, have subsequently tried to reform the image of the game in order to relaunch it for television, with all the rewards it would bring to them. Snooker has not suffered in this extreme way, indeed it remains important enough for satellite television to bid for coverage rights; but audiences have declined massively over the last decade. That the hierarchy of sport is not permanent makes another important point about the power of television, to which we will return in Chapter Five: powerful as it is, television cannot simply create and maintain a sporting public. It is through the media as a whole that the public as a whole is acquainted with this hierarchised world of sport, addressed as local and national consumers of it, and through it that many of them make sense of it – or refuse its meaning altogether, which is always an option with any imagined community with which one does not have to (indeed, one cannot) deal directly. Yet, powerful as the media are, their messages are modified and sometimes refused outright by their consumers.

One very important question arising from this powerful form of address, the media, concerns the place of women. The new team sports emerged in and through a culture of male participation which was if anything reinforced when they were taken up by the working class. Any sport reworked through the middle-class codes of discipline and honour, whose aim was the creation of a ruling élite, tended to exclude women as participants, and many sports also actively discouraged women as observers. However, many schools for girls took up sports – though this included gentler practices such as Laban movement and Swedish gymnastics, which while physically taxing lacked the person-to-person aggression of team sports.[1] Physical education for girls was often organised around the idea of health and fitness, rather than personal, team or school victory – though at many schools girls also played hockey, cricket, and arguably the most violent of all the team sports, lacrosse.[2] However, the dominant narrative both of female bodily health and of the schools' preparation of their pupils for life after school was of domestic femininity (as was the representation of female stars: one newspaper headline after Fanny Blankers-Koen had won her fourth medal at the 1948 Olympics read FASTEST WOMAN IN THE WORLD IS EXPERT COOK; her motherhood was also stressed).[3] Women were actively discouraged from competitive sport outside the school playing field. Events at the Olympics were only opened to women in 1908, and even then women were restricted to events considered (by men) to be physically suitable (archery, tennis, and figure skating); when competitors collapsed after the finish of a 800 metre race at the 1928 finals, it was argued that middle- and long-distance running would be too 'dangerous', that the female body would be damaged irreparably by competition. Other sports, such as shooting, were considered 'unfeminine': it was only opened to women in 1984. Even now some Olympic events, such as throwing the hammer, are restricted to male participants only.[4]

No women's team sport developed as a mass spectator sport in the way that association football did in the twentieth century; only in lawn tennis, from the inter-war years, was there audience demand which meant high ticket sales. This in turn paved the way for the beginnings of equal financial treatment for women participants (though even here equality of prize money is not achieved in all tournaments), and more recently there have been fully professional American and European golf circuits, complete with sponsorship; of team sports, women's cricket in the Caribbean and India has achieved mass spectatorship in recent years, and women's soccer has a professional league in Italy (and over half a million amateur players in Germany; it is the fastest-growing participant sport in France). This comparative lack of public support is not, of course, because women were unwilling to participate in sports, or to perform to a high enough standard, or because all women think that sport is a silly male activity; they were actively prevented from taking part in it. Working-class women were barred from entry to snooker clubs; middle-class women were barred from entry to golf clubs (many golf clubs in Britain, despite equal opportunities legislation, are still male-only, and allow women only as 'lady' associate members, unable to vote at general meetings or play at certain times of the week, or worse still, 'lady guests' only allowed in the clubhouse with a man. The patronising restriction implied by that very Victorian construction, the 'lady', implying female physical weakness, is a crucial aspect of the language of bourgeois sport). In the 1970s, a series of bizarre rulings in the British courts overrode existing equal opportunities legislation and allowed the Football Association to forbid the presence of girls in under-12 football teams playing in its competitions. This decision was finally reversed in 1988.

These exclusions are often justified with recourse to biological arguments. It has been argued that women are frail, and unsuited to fierce competition, because they menstruate and bear children. The argument is ridiculous. One comprehensive survey found that 22 per cent of female athletes actually performed better during their periods, as against 34 per cent who did worse. Many women, such as the middle-distance runner Liz MColgan, have actually increased their performances, returning better times, after giving birth. Far more vulnerable is the male body, with its unprotected exterior genitals asking to be crushed in the scrum or against the saddle, or smashed to a pulp by a cricket ball (which is why batsmen wear an aluminium 'box' as part of their body armour).[5] There is a more subtle biological argument against equal participation. Women are *on average* smaller, have less muscle bulk even after training, and have smaller lung capacities. Their ability to produce instant energy is therefore lower. However, women have higher fat reserves which allow them to compete more equally against men in very long-distance events such as channel swimming and long distance running. One important statistic remains constant. In all athletic sports, women's performances are improving on a faster curve than men's. Some calculations predict that women will regularly beat men in events such as the marathon within thirty years, and in shorter distance races within fifty.[6]

As Chapter Five will argue, the very notion of gender equality may by that time seem somewhat antiquated. There is, however, another set of arguments about gender and its construction which move away from the purely biological – or, at least, from the world of performance and measurement. This is the claim that there is a qualitatively different world of women's sports, a world which de-emphasises the aggressive competitiveness of 'malestream' sport, and which instead emphasises fitness and health, lightness and grace of movement.

From this point of view, arguably the most important sports through which women can become part of the sport-imagined world have been gymnastics, ice dance and equestrian sports like show-jumping and the three-day event. In equestrianism, where the muscles are the horse's, women compete as the equals of men and as often win the top prizes; in all equestrian events, but particularly the dressage part of the three-day event, horse and rider can achieve a 'natural' balance which is a world away from the competitive brutality of the rugby tackle. Aesthetic judgments are necessary for the award of victory. In gymnastics, similarly, women are seen to be the star performers, because they combine precision with grace and beauty of movement – though the effects of this athletic glamour on those who wish to perform themselves can be very dangerous. The pre-pubescent body (sometimes maintained in that state by drugs) and the physical risks of the routines on floor and bars are a frightening combination.

Ice dance rose to fame in Britain because of the international success of British performers, notably John Curry and the duo of Jayne Torville and Christopher Dean. The British media attention to the sport since Torville and Dean's decline (and their failure to win gold in the 1992 Winter Olympics) has lessened, though it still receives more exposure than darts. Synchronised swimming is another sport which women have practised rather more than men – and as with ice dance and gymnastics, men have often argued that because the stress is on beauty rather than competitive aggression, it should not be treated as a sport; its current Olympic status as a 'demonstration' sport rather than one for which medals are awarded, confirms this masculine view. The current campaign to make competitive aerobics into a full Olympic sport underlines the way in which many women want to see themselves as sportswomen – as in command of fluidly aestheticised bodily movement as well as fit and athletic. Again, here is a sport to which many women are drawn by its grace, beauty and glamour, its refusal of what they see as the masculine values of other sporting activities: through this combination they too can become drawn into the matrix of personal, local, national and global meaning which is available to men through sport. The Olympic accolade for aerobics would be a powerful and welcome assertion of this feminisation of the values of sport.

Many women, however, have simply no point of contact with sport. Given their systematic exclusion from most forms of participation in sport and its associated social activities, it is not surprising that many women evince hostility to sport in all its forms. In what is clearly a circular problem, they are, therefore, not addressed by the mass of the sporting media. There are comparatively few female sports reporters. Most of their male colleagues implicitly address a clubbable male world when they discuss sporting matters. Women are implicitly, sometimes explicitly, excluded from these versions of the local and the national. The nation as defined through sporting activity and its media presentation, the public world of sport, is overwhelmingly a male nation. Again, the resonances of the argument about hunting and the public sphere seem obvious here – though it is worth pointing out that women have been active participants in fox-hunting since the middle of the nineteenth century.

Similar problems of exclusion affect the peoples who are currently characterised as 'ethnic minorities'. People from the dispersed nations, such as Jews, Afro-Caribbeans and African Americans, Indians and Chinese are to be found in most parts of Europe and the United States: existing in these racist societies, it is difficult for them to fit into 'grand narratives' of sporting nationality which often systematically exclude them. Where some barriers fall, others usually continue to exist. Black Americans were excluded from participation in professional sport until the 1940s. They are now successful as players in all areas of American sport; yet there are still very few black coaches or managers. The situation is similar in Britain, where the success of athletes like Tessa Sanderson and Daley Thompson has not yet been matched by the emergence of black coaches in proportionate numbers. This could be a generational problem (the presence of large numbers of black British people only dates back to the 1950s); certainly there are more black coaching staff in soccer currently, in the 1990s, than there were a decade ago, partly because the 1980s were the first decade of large-scale black participation in professional British soccer.

How then do black American or British people experience the address into the imagined community which sport provides? How are they 'hailed into position'? No doubt the situation is easier after the Barcelona Olympic Games, when, for instance, a basketball team consisting entirely of black American players won an Olympic title, and when a black British sprinter won the Olympic 100 metres, and all involved are acclaimed by the media as unproblematically representatives of their nation – as 'heroes'. And in some ways, as I argued in Chapter One, this does indeed signal that the narrative of the imagined community has produced a change, as narratives do, and that the story told by sport is that black people are indeed full citizens of their respective countries. Yet black people are often in a position to see the problems in this construction and to deny its magic. The boxer Cassius Clay won a gold medal for the USA at the 1964 Olympics. After a store owner in his home town refused to serve him because of the colour of his skin, he threw the medal away; this rejection of what the USA was is as important a denial as Clay's later embrace of Islam under the title Muhammad Ali. Many would argue that the position of black sports performers as heroes denies the real position of most blacks in western countries – that it is a particularly insidious form of 'false consciousness'.

A particular question arises for the 'ethnic minority' population when sportspeople from their or their parent's former homes visit their new countries. How do their loyalties lie – and how should they? Which player or team should they support? Outraged by vociferous support from British residents for a touring cricket team from Pakistan, the British Conservative politician Norman Tebbit claimed that immigrants should take the 'Tebbit Cricket Test' – with the clear implication that if they chose to support the team representing their former homeland, they should return there. A drop in the support for West Indian touring cricket teams in Britain suggests that, perhaps because people of West Indian extraction now occasionally represent England at cricket, many British West Indians would now 'pass' the 'Tebbit test'. It could also be argued, however, that despite the success of individual black athletes, most black people still experience racism, and younger people in particular reject every aspect of the dominant culture, including the imperial sports which their parents and grandparents practised in the Caribbean. They reject the sporting version of imagined Englishness, along with everything else. But it is not only people from communities of recent immigrants for whom sport provides conflicts of loyalty.

The Supporter and the Fan

All definitions and forms of identity within fandom are changing rapidly. The rise of new-technology based interactive games, which have threatened (perhaps even replaced) the thirty year primacy of popular music as a formant of identity within youth cultures, is producing a new kind of games consciousness which will no doubt have an impact on fans and their dreams and desires; it will therefore have an impact on the sports they wish to view or participate in in the near future.

Between the general public and the fan there is a huge gulf of perception, though there is an intermediate level, a category I identify here as the supporter, to whom sports are an important, enjoyable, but part-time leisure pursuit and not the centre of life's meaning. A supporter will usually practise sports at school and for some time thereafter, and will often support the sport he or she has played, going on to be an observer, official, or club member. A supporter may attend sports on a regular or irregular basis, and will be informed of her or his chosen team's or player's performance through the local and national media. The team's or player's success will be welcome, and failure will not; either will affect their mood, and their work: one study of Italian car workers, at the

FIAT factory in Turin, showed that their productivity fell in the days after the local football team, Juventus, was defeated, and rose (despite the probability of intoxicating celebrations) after an important victory. The managing director of FIAT owned Juventus and invested heavily in its players, for this very reason. Supporters, however, often claim to have other interests. So although much of what I say about the fan also applies to the supporter, there are real differences which must be addressed.

With the fan (the obsessively dedicated follower of particular sports, teams and/or players) the difference from the supporter is perhaps only one of degree. I should stress that I do not use the term obsession as meaning abnormal; there is nothing unusual about this kind of interest. In an extraordinary book called *Crack Wars*, the writer Avital Ronell argued – I think correctly – that our society is characterised by addiction.[7] For Ronell, intense, repeated craving is a normal aspect of our psychology. I would argue that fans who are addicted to their teams, players and sports are expressing this psychological deep structure in the same way as devotees of types of music or particular musicians, or of genres of literature like romance or detective fiction, or indeed like drug addicts. To say again: this is normal, and while fans are usually aware that the intensity of their devotion sets them apart from a notional general public or casual sports supporters, they do not consider themselves psychotic in any generally or personally harmful sense, but will often quite happily admit to their obsession.[8]

This is not to say that obsession is all good clean fun. Referees, officials, managers and officials have all been attacked by fanatical followers of sports. After their 6–1 defeat in Montreal in 1978, members of the Indian men's hockey team returned to find not a hero's welcome but an illuminated address: their houses had been burned down by angry crowds.[9] In July 1994 the Colombian footballer Andres Escobar was shot dead in Bogota, following his team's surprisingly early exit from the summer's World Cup finals. He had scored the own goal which had allowed the unfancied United States team the victory: it was assumed that he had been killed by someone who had lost money in betting on the outcome of the match, but it could as easily have been by someone who felt patriotically challenged by the defeat. On 30 April 1993, the tennis player Monica Seles was attacked by a fan as she played a championship match in Hamburg. Seles was stabbed in the upper back, and was taken to hospital. She was expected to be physically able to play again in six months but in fact the necessity for psychological rehabilitation delayed her return to competitive tennis for two years. Her attacker claimed to be a follower of one of her rivals on the circuit, Stefi Graf; he had, apparently, attacked Seles in order to give Graf a better chance of winning the tournament.

Although many fans are socialised as members of a fan community through the media, these are very different media from the national and local services for which sport is only a part, however important, of the news scene. Even so, sports supporters and fans alike can and do read newspapers – they just read them in the 'wrong' direction, as sport-centred. As Stuart Hall argued in a perceptive article on football hooliganism, you do this by by treating the back page, with its lead story and headline, as if it were the front.[10] Most newspapers, including broadsheets, can very easily be read in this way; it is certainly my own experience of newspaper reading. But the specialised media are more important to the fan. For most professional sports, there are dedicated journals, weekly and monthly magazines and even daily newspapers, such as the *Sporting Life* in England, which deals mainly with horse racing, and the soccer-based *Gazzetto dello Sport* in Italy. There are similar radio and television programmes, even full-time networks in some places. For media products like these, as for many of their readers, listeners and viewers, their sport, and their team or player within it, is not part of a totality; it *is* the totality, or at least its centre, and the whole of life is seen from its perspective. This is as true of the commercial publications as of the fanzines, which are dedicated to individual clubs or players, and produced by fans rather than profit-seeking companies. The centre of this imagined community is not even the game or its structure, but the team, or the special player. The rest of the imagined community is first and foremost other fans, people who share this very special perspective: fellow addicts – or perhaps one should say fellow believers.

The comparisons with religious expression, and especially
with small-scale religious groups and cults, are obvious, but
none the less convincing for that. While the casual watcher
or the supporter may treat the experience of attending a
sports tournament as the equivalent of an evening meal at a
restaurant, or a night at the pub, or a visit to the theatre, to
the fan entering the stadium is entering a shrine. The
supporter is there to support; the fan to worship. Guttmann's insistence that one prime defining term for modern
sport is 'secularisation' cannot stand examination through
the eyes of the truly dedicated fan.

Given these basic differences, it is not surprising that the
world is a very different place for a fan than for a member
of the general public, or even for a supporter; hardly
surprising that the fan is notoriously difficult to treat as a
political animal. Having worked out a comprehension of
their particular sport through a matrix of obsessive affiliation, the fan will only be roused if the centre of that matrix
is directly threatened – the departure of a favourite player
from a team, or a threat to the established structure of the
game from a change in ownership and responsibility, or a
threat to that person's ability to carry on worshipping at the
shrine such as a hike in entrance charges. In the case of
association football in England, the persistence of football
hooliganism from the 1960s onwards elicited no united
opposition from other people who watched football, for all
that they insisted that they were the 'real' supporters (and
therefore somehow different from the hooligans).

Whether or not there was an identifiably separate
category of football fan-not-hooligan, the Government
came increasingly to the view that all football supporters
should be treated, badly, under one category. Riots instigated by English fans in Europe in the early 1980s had
provoked ministerial outrage (though this puzzled some of
the arrested fans, who claimed convincingly that their
arrogant, ignorant hatred of all foreigners merely matched
that of the prime minister and her minions). The Government was finally spurred into action, however, after a
domestic dispute which was directly related to the most
important political confrontation of the 1980s: the miners'
strike.

In 1974 strikes by the miners had led to the fall of the

Conservative government. During 1984–5 the miners tried to repeat the dose. Some of their number, however, refused to join the stoppage, and as a result there were mass pickets at some coalfields. Against this perceived intimidation, the Government used the police as a paramilitary force. Mounted police were seen on television charging into the pickets and scattering them in disarray. To the opponents of the Government this looked uncommonly like fascism. To its supporters, it was the long overdue judgment of God (in Her guise, usual on these occasions, as a middle-class Englishman) on a consensual political system which had long outlived its usefulness.

Meanwhile, Millwall Football Club had embarked on a good run in the most prestigious British soccer competition, the FA Cup. Millwall's fans have always had a reputation for violent hostility to opposing supporters. Their heritage in London Docklands marked them as rough, but comparatively wealthy, working-class; their rough reputation was reinforced by a television programme broadcast in the autumn of 1977 in the BBC's Panorama series of investigative documentaries. Entitled 'The F Troop, Treatment, and the Half-Way Line', this programme presented first the 'F-Troop', a bunch of middle-aged fans under the leadership of the quaintly named Harry the Dog. One of them claimed to have pulled out of his wedding at the last minute in order to attend an away match, and all said they had regularly used their fists in the cause of the club. 'Treatment' turned out to be a group of youngish men who claimed to go looking for trouble wearing surgical masks in order to hand out 'the treatment' to all in their way. The 'half-way line' was a motley group of young teenagers and boys who clearly saw themselves as apprentices for the older groups, who seemed to hate all other teams and their fans, and who couldn't wait to get stuck in alongside their elders. Needless to say much of this was a boastful wind-up of a rather naive young, middle-class journalist. But the reputation of the club's supporters grew nonetheless, and was reinforced by the adoption of a self-parodic anthem: to the lugubrious melody of Rod Stewart's rock anthem 'Sailing', the Millwall fans would sing 'No-one Likes Us,

We Don't Care, We Are Millwall, From the Den'. Carnival
and the reversal of routine values indeed.

   Those who wished to identify with this label flocked to
the Millwall banner as their 1985 cup run proceeded. In
the sixth round of the competition they were drawn
against First Division Luton Town, a club with its best-ever
team, but comparatively few and docile supporters, and a
police force very eager to protect them. The first attempt
to settle the tie, a game at Millwall, was drawn. Luton won
the replay on their own ground by two goals to nil. When
the police locked them inside the ground for half an hour
after the match had ended, in order to allow home
supporters to get away in safety, the Millwall fans packed
onto the visitors' terrace, whose disquiet at their team's
subdued performance had been increasingly apparent,
rioted. In full view of the television cameras, the police
charged, as their mounted colleagues had charged the
miners. The Millwall fans were having none of it; they
counter-charged; and the police bravely ran away. The
subsequent rebuilding of the police line and their
counter-counter-charge which did, eventually, restore
order have not become the stuff of legend. The watching
public, including watching Government Ministers, were
treated to action replays of the Millwall fans' temporary
triumph.

   It was in my view this event, and not the subsequent
disasters at Bradford and Heysel, which led to Mrs
Thatcher's decision to 'do something', in her thankfully
inimitable way: though the later events provided pretext
and justification. The Government's proposed remedy was
the draconian Football Spectator's (Membership) Bill,
whose chief provision was to require every football
supporter to sign up as a member of one named club,
which would provide a credit-card type membership card.
Only this electronically traceable card would be used to
gain entrance to a football ground. Misbehavers would
when arrested and convicted be deprived of their cards,
and hey presto! No more football hooligans. Sadly, no
more casual supporters, able to decide of a Saturday 'let's
go to a football match this afternoon'. And incidentally, no
more visiting supporters, for clubs who did not want them
– or the associated policing bills. Luton Town had anyway,

perhaps understandably, instigated a ban of their own on visiting supporters.

It was the threat to their obsession represented by the Football Spectator's Bill which finally galvanised the docile spectators into action. Opposition to the Bill focussed an already nascent football fanzine subculture, helped to form a nationwide football supporters' association, and provided the stimulus to further academic research on football and its place – including the setting up of the Football Research Unit at Leicester University. Though only indirectly responsible for the failure of the Football Spectator's Bill (which was withdrawn after Lord Justice Taylor's report on the Hillsborough disaster pointed out that electronically controlled gates were a safety hazard) the new articulacy did have positive effects.[11]

Since this campaign the followers of most football clubs have become politicised – they have taken a far more vocal interest in the affairs of 'their' clubs. The typical independent supporter's association came into being when a favourite part of a football ground was threatened with redevelopment, and then remained in being to fight the owners of the club on a more general basis – while remaining fiercely loyal to their perception of the club itself: its players and coaching staff.

For the fan, then, the form of national identity offered to the general public through sporting activities can be severely compromised by the particular affiliation, perceived community and sense of belonging offered by the status of fan. Like the team players, fans of teams from metropolitan areas are often from a mixture of nationalities, ethnicities, religious and political cultures: there are many Greek, Irish, Jewish and Afro-Caribbean followers of the North London soccer team Arsenal: certainly no common sense of 'Tebbit Test' loyalty can be expected from them at international level. Even where these conflicts do not exist, given the risks of injury and more general tiredness, fans may not want 'their' players to play for national teams, and may not transfer their loyalties to national sporting representatives: so team games may produce certain types of national identity, but they can and in the late twentieth century increasingly often do confuse or refuse them. Metropolitan identities in particular are so diffuse now that even the category 'national capital' would seem a misnomer.

Fan identity is not uniform, even across different teams playing the same sport. Some fans' matrix of meaning leans heavily on the teams of the past, their successes or near-successes, or the legendary exploits of former players. Other fans have a cult of the fan, one which sees the existence of the team sport as the (almost incidental) stage on which they strut: they characterise themselves as the best, the most dedicated, the most vocal, the most knowledgeable, or even the most aggressive, supporters. Again, given the choice between success (the winning of trophies) and stylish performance, the fans of some teams will insist on success at any price, including cheating by their own team, while the fans of other teams will opt for style, as it is part of their matrix of meaning – the performance tradition of some clubs is more important than individual players, and even than the record of trophies won: it differentiates teams and their fans. To win without style would be to lower their team, and by implication themselves, to the others' level. In soccer, rugby and cricket debates continue about the best way to play the game – debates whose aesthetic implications will be confronted in Chapter Seven.

Having introduced 'the Treatment', this is perhaps the most obvious place to discuss the 'football hooligan', that mad beast of the terraces so hated by the press. This is the one area of sports studies with a large literature in sociology and closely related work in cultural studies, so while the temptation to review it in detail must be resisted, a general sketch of the changing nature of this investigation will be outlined.

In the 1960s and early 1970s the phenomenon was viewed apologetically by academics, who saw themselves as on the side of the working class, and 'hooliganism' as an almost harmless aspect of working-class adolescence.[12] It was claimed that what appeared to be violent confrontation was in fact highly ritualised; very few people actually got hurt. This view was unsustainable. The deaths at Heysel Stadium, which followed an escalation of violent incidents by English football followers abroad, finally led to a more realistic approach: this form of organised male violence was as sordid as any other, and even academics felt obliged to propose policy initiatives to curtail it.[13] What is clear from their empirical work is that while some hooligans are not dedicated football followers in the way that fans are, and only care for the rituals of violence, others are fans, genuinely interested in the fortunes of their teams, who also like a fight.[14] It is just as difficult to generalise about hooligans' social backgrounds or work experience. Clearly, however, their notions of imagined community – of the localities and nations they are fighting for – are very well developed. Many commentators noted that the growth of English fans' aggression abroad occurred after the Falklands War had, apparently, restored national pride. Arrested after incidents in Spain, many English hooligans expressed shock at hearing Margaret Thatcher's condemnation of them. As far as they were concerned, they were fighting for Britain in the same way, and with the same values, as the Prime Minister.

A similar phenomenon was the export of British 'lager louts' to Spanish holiday resorts like Marbella. British holidaymakers were notorious for their consumption of alcohol and their propensity to violence. In these Spanish resorts, however, a movement started which, according to one group of academics at Manchester Metropolitan University, has transformed the culture both of nightclubs and the football terraces. The Manchester monitors claim that 'rave' culture, based on dance music and the drug Ecstasy, has brought about a more passive fan culture, even among young men. The two cultures of dance and football have interacted, producing a new kind of imagined community to undermine the aggression which was threatening the future of football. Fanzines and the people who read them have combatted racism and sexism within the game rather than accepting it.[15] It's probably too early to say whether this optimism holds water (certainly the reporting of violent soccer-related incidents has declined, though it has not disappeared); but one has to be thankful that some academics at least are taking the relation between sport and the rest of society seriously.

One problem with this approach, as with virtually all sociology and cultural studies work on youth culture, is precisely that it is about youth. This category may well have been exciting in the 1950s or even the 1960s; now, it is old hat. The population of western Europe is aging; the 'subversive' potential of youth never did hold out any hope for the future, and it holds even less now that youth is an increasingly small minority. Sport, likewise, has to be rethought in the light of the changing concerns of the aging public.[16] This does not mean abandoning sport as a public spectacle. Many professional sports now operate a parallel circuit, in which professional players of the over-forties continue to perform in public, and to entertain the public which had watched them in their physical 'prime'. Even the meaning of this category has come under increasing threat; the body, in the late twentieth century, is beginning to escape from the grand narrative of aging. This widening of the physical boundaries of public sport may well help to keep an older population interested; it will also have effects on the way that players see themselves, and it is to this complex form of identity that we now turn.

Identity, the Public and the Player

The forces operating on the participant spectator are of course not the same as those of the participant player or performer. Here we must first confront another important paradox in the relationship between sport and nation. Many players, perhaps most at the very top levels of their sports, do not pursue their calling in the localities or even the countries of their birth: by and large, they perform for the highest bidder, and how and when that bidder requires. The highlight of many a boxer's career, for example, is a fight in Las Vegas, which may well be fought early in the morning to maximise worldwide television exposure – which is far better for the boxer's purse than for his ability to function biologically and athletically. Professional cricketers from all over the world play in the English county game and for the Lancashire and Yorkshire Leagues, which are the only sectors of the game outside the international circus currently to offer a living. Golfers and tennis players play the tournaments with the highest prize money, even if that means the inconvenience of continually flying around the world, living without the rootedness of home or family. In world football, the highest wages are earned in Spain and Italy; therefore, the best players in the world, and the best club sides on the continent, tend to be in Spain and Italy: were it not for European regulations preventing the playing of 'foreign' players in inter-European cup competitions, even more would play in southern Europe. This does not necessarily prevent players from representing their countries, but it creates a particularly severe version of the conflict between club and country when a player might be expected to play a match, fly-half way round the world – say from Italy to Argentina – in order to play international football, and then to fly back again immediately for another domestic league match. Not surprisingly, there is a tendency for clubs to claim that the players in whom they invest such huge sums are injured, and cannot be released for international matches.

Quite what the players themselves make of this is unclear, though there is an emerging tendency for players and their advisors to plan a career which involves several changes of club in order to maximise earning potential through a series of transfer fees (from which the player usually earns a percentage). Obviously one of the most important focusing points for the identity of the contemporary sports performer is money; where there is a conflict between country and the chance to earn money, many players will choose money. Tennis players have refused to represent America in Davis Cup matches where they could earn more elsewhere.

Cricket provides perhaps the clearest example of this mercenary tendency. For all its importance as a national and international icon within the Commonwealth, cricket was a poorly paid sport, even at international level, in the early 1970s. When the Australian television entrepreneur Kerry Packer was refused television rights for Australian cricket, he set up his own competition called World Series cricket. As the title implies, this was an Americanisation of the sport, reliant on the hard sell of a confrontation between fast bowlers and aggressive batsmen (cricket helmets and other body armour date from the Packer series), and emphasising the instant entertainment of the one-day international rather than the cumulative pleasures and tensions of the five-day Test match. World Series cricket also cut across the existing local, national and international playing arrangements by assembling a multinational side with players from South Africa, New Zealand, England, Pakistan and India to play against 'national' teams from Australia and West Indies. Match fees were far higher than anything cricketers had previously enjoyed. Despite the loss of international caps, and the severe disfavour of their local cricket bureaucracies, many of the world's best players signed up with Packer. Similarly, cricketers from Australia, West Indies and England made well-paid tours of apartheid South Africa despite the opposition of their cricketing authorities and governments. Not all players pocketed the large sums offered by Packer, or by South Africa: enough did so, however, to throw into doubt the idea that somehow players are so 'naturally' proud to play for 'their' country that such pride will outweigh other considerations.

The quotation marks around 'their' are important. Since the brief moment of Packer's circus, in fact, there has also been an increasing tendency for players to play Test (and one-day international) cricket for 'adopted' countries, rather than those of their birth. South Africans (who from 1970 until 1992 were prevented from playing international cricket for South Africa) have played for Australia and England; a Pakistani for New Zealand; a New Zealander and an Australian opened the bowling for an England team against Australia in 1993 ('England' lost). Oddly enough, in July 1995 *Wisden* cricket magazine published an article by one Robert Henderson, which seemed (the author denied it) to put forward the racist argument that players not born in England, and/or not white, would not perform at their best for England. Several black players who have represented England sued for libel, and won. Of course, the crude argument is nonsense; but in a world dominated by international television and in which national allegiance can be bought, 'loyalty' to a national side containing people born and raised in several different countries, *and* people eager to play for the highest bidder, is at least a topic for discussion.

The tendency is not limited to cricket: Western Samoans

have played rugby for New Zealand, and many players with only the most tenuous genetic connections have played football for the Republic of Ireland. Many foreign born players turned out for the United States in the 1994 soccer World Cup team which, like the England cricket team of the 1980s and beyond, needed all the help it could get. This tendency indicates something very important about both the identity of the contemporary sports player in the era of professionalism, and the nature of both capital and nationality in the world at the end of the twentieth century. For now the point to stress is that most professional players of team games are born into the working class, but the immense wealth conferred by sporting success means that they do not stay in it (for all the attempts by some, such as the footballer Paul Gascoigne, to live a parody of working-class masculinity). Their subjectivity changes, and both to themselves and to spectators they therefore lose some of the iconic identity which international representation once conferred on players as much as on the participant spectator, and on the observing media. For the players, then, nation, sport and identity are no longer automatically conflated: when media commentators lament sporting failure as a signal of national decline, they should perhaps be asking whether or not, for the players who live in a declassed, polyglot world divorced from more normal ties to nationality, region and career, 'nation' remains a meaningful term.

There are other important formants through which the professional performer can construct an identity: one, arguably more important and more stable than notions of representation, is the idea of the career. Players are graded by ability, and first directed towards a professional career at school, or by their parents (as in the case of tennis players such as Boris Becker, and most notoriously Mary Pierce, whose father's aggressive attitude to his daughter and her career has led to his being banned from competitions in which she plays). They are then directed towards coaching schemes and other forms of apprentice-ship at junior clubs, or colleges, before being taken on by professional clubs or joining the professional circuit. They will usually have a few years in which to make the breakthrough to a regular team place or regular prize money, and thereafter a dozen years or so (more in the case of golf or snooker) in which to shine at their profession. This can then be added to in many sports by the adoption of a post-performance career in sports management, coaching, administration or journalism; increasingly, as mentioned above, there is also the prospect of post-prime performance.

The sporting career is aspirational; fantasies of success drive young performers in every activity. They are fantasies which in most cases will lead to disappointment. Several sociologists and historians have claimed that the fantasy is particularly contradictory in relation to black performers, where there is a myth of sports success as a way out of relative deprivation. It is a myth based on highly visible models. In the United States and Britain, the achievement of black athletes in recent years has offered a powerful model to young black people who feel that they will otherwise be constrained by their surroundings to lives of under-achievement. Former Wimbledon champion Arthur Ashe, one of those role models, was very concerned at its negative impact, and campaigned for young black people to be given models of middle-class professional success. Sociologists Ellis Cashmore and Stephen Reiss have argued that the myth leads to many young black people investing heavily in sport, to the detriment of schoolwork; a very few succeed, but most will not become professional performers (according to Reiss, there were only 624 registered professional baseball players in the USA in 1988).[17] Even those who do succeed usually have short careers; only a minority then become involved in coaching and other lucrative post-performance careers. The story of Joe Louis, a former world heavyweight boxing champion who died in poverty, underlines the point. By this argument, black athletic success actually helps to reproduce underachievement among black people.

For the successful athlete, the career means more to the individual than just the movement through time, from apprenticeship through prime to declining power: it means a series of relationships with other individuals – other team or circuit members, managers and coaches, fans and supporters. These people will all address the player as a particular member of the sporting unit: say a quarterback or wide receiver in American football. They will offer advice or give instructions as to the performance of that particular role, advice which helps to form the player's notion of how to perform that role, and which can be used to form a model against which the player can understand her or his own performance as success or failure. This does not necessarily just mean in terms of victory or defeat. Many coaches are obsessive statisticians, as are many fans, and will award accolades only to the performer who makes more home runs, or takes more wickets, than previous generations of players in the same position. To this mentality, a career is an aggregate of such statistics; a final average. Other fans, and some coaches, will also judge performance by particular aesthetic standards, arguing that the best players are those who execute the movements appropriate to their sport with grace and beauty, or excessive power, not just point-scoring effectiveness.

Another recent formant of identity for the professional player is the relationship with her or his agent. Here the player will constantly be addressed as someone with massive, but usually only short to medium term, earning potential. This will necessarily mean pursuing employing clubs to increase earnings from contracts; it may also mean negotiating with sports goods manufacturers or other commercial firms for sponsorships or endorsements. Such sums do not automatically follow from performance success, however. The basketball player Michael Jordan was reckoned to earn $30 million per year from endorsement deals in 1992-3 season. However, revelations towards the end of the season that Jordan had a 'gambling problem' put some of these deals in jeopardy, despite his leading his team to its third successive World Series championship. Having managed to be simultaneously lionised as champion and scapegoated as gambler, Jordan quit basketball soon after that last World Series, and passed his time for the next year in minor league baseball.

The example of Michael Jordan should remind us that players often have an uneasy relationship with the public. At both the national and international level, this relationship is mediated by a press which is always hungry for stories about 'stars', and will discuss a sporting hero(ine)'s sexuality or taste in designer drugs as easily as it will discuss her or his performance on the field of play. Behaviour presented by the media as aberrant or excessive will lead to public censure which in some cases then rebounds on the player's earning ability; tennis star Martina Navratilova's lesbianism has, it is claimed, cost her millions of dollars in potential earnings. Navratilova complained that basketball player Magic Johnson's revelation that his AIDS had been contacted through one or more of thousands of heterosexual conquests had led to sympathy rather than censure. Even in an America increasingly influenced by the religious right, the agreed version of heterosexual masculinity still allows the double standard, and sporting heroism encompasses that standard. Much of players' positive self-view comes from their contact with particular fans; much of their negative view from this contact with wider publics mediated by press, radio and television reporting which judges them against a set of norms which it assumes are shared by the national, local and international publics whom the players are taken to represent.

For any player at the top level in international sport, there is no 'private' life in the sense in which it is understood by most of us. They are public icons just as monarchs and film stars are public icons, and they are judged not against our own standards but against those of the imagined community; judged against publicly agreed norms of conduct, but also against our dreams, our fantasies and desires. This is as true off the field as it is on it.

Notes

1. S. Fletcher, 'The Making and Breaking of a Female Tradition: Women's Physical Education in England 1880-1980', in J.A. Mangan and R.J. Park (eds), *From 'Fair Sex' to Feminism. Sport and the Socialization of Women in the Industrial and Post-Industrial Eras*, Frank Cass, London 1987, pp145-157.

2. K.E. McCrone, 'Play up! Play up! and Play the Game! Sport at the late Victorian Girls' Public Schools', in Mangan and Parks (eds), *From 'Fair Sex' to Feminism*, pp97-129.

3. A. Blue, *op.cit.*, p72.

4. Jennifer Hargreaves, *op.cit.*, pp209-234.

5. See the amusing essay by A. Blue, 'An Immodest Proposal', in *Citius Fortius Altius*, The Design Museum, February 1990, pp37-43.

6. These arguments and their supporting statistics can be found in Dyer, *Catching up the Men*.

7. A. Ronnell, *Crack Wars: Literature Addiction Mania*, University of Nebraska Press, 1992. See review by A. Blake, 'Cultured Addicts and Cyberpunks', *The Times Higher Education Supplement*, July 24, 1992.

8. Some interesting consideration of fans and popular culture which completely ignored sports, is the collection edited by L.A. Lewis, *The Adoring Audience: Fan Culture and Popular Media*, Routledge, 1992.

9. Honesty box: I owe my phrasing here to a self-deprecatory remark in a radio interview given by former soccer manager Tommy Docherty.

10. S. Hall, 'The Treatment of "Football Hooliganism" in the Press', in Ingham *et al.*, *Football Hooliganism*.

11. A similar scheme in Holland was abandoned after one week, due to the non-co-operation of crowds: B. Houlihan, *The Government and Politics of Sport*, pp193.

12. P. Marsh, E. Rosser, R. Harre, *The Rules of Disorder*, Routledge Kegan Paul, London 1978.

13. J. Williams *et al.*, *op.cit.*

14. See B. Buford, *Among the Thugs*, Secker and Warburg, London 1991; C. Ward, *Steaming In: Journal of a Football Fan* (Sportspages/Simon and Schuster 1989; R. Turner, *In Your Blood: Football Culture in the Late 1980s and early 1990s*, Working Press, 1991.

15. See S. Redhead, *Football with Attitude*, Wordsmith, Manchester 1991; Redhead (ed), *The Passion and the Fashion*, Avebury, Aldershot, 1994.

16. See A. Blake, 'Britische Jugend: Gibt es Noch? (British Youth: Does it Still Exist?)', in R. Horak and N. Bailer (eds), *Jugendkultur, Annäherungen*, WUV Universitatsverlag, Vienna, 1995.

17. E. Cashmore, *Black Sportsmen*, Routledge, London 1982; S. Reiss, 'Professional Sports as an Avenue of Social Mobility in America: Some Myths and Realities', in D.G. Kyle and G.D. Stark, (eds), *Essays on Sport History and Sport Mythology*, Texas University Press, 1990, pp84-111.

5 The Body Language: Designing the Performer

I stay with the identity (and more particularly with the body) of the player in order to address the questions of technology and capital. Many players are in some ways simply the representatives, even the products, of technological and biochemical developments; the body of the athlete is no longer (if it ever was) a self-contained biological unit. Does this mean that the athlete is, as Jean-Marie Brohm suggested, merely the dupe of the capitalist system, providing both profit for the owners of the team or the equipment-maker and an example of personal or team dedication and discipline for workers elsewhere to emulate? Can we see athletes, however highly paid, as dupes, or even as victims?

While this assumption, as with most attempts to blame capitalism for everything, is far too simple, it begins to unlock a fertile area of debate about sport, its potential futures, and those of humanity in general. This is not to deny the importance of capital in the direction of competitive professional sport – or that in many cases the athlete seems to be the servant of the equipment, rather than the other way round. An important current debate in many sports concerns the relationship between the body and the equipment necessary (or claimed to be necessary) for performance. This question is often debated because of apparent changes in the ways games are played, and particularly because of apparent changes for the worse.

It has come to attention recently that professional men's tennis depends more on strength than on the subtler skills of technique, placement and anticipation of the opponent's movements. The rallying game has gone, especially on grass courts, as a series of well-built men serve as fast as possible. The ball is hardly ever in play for more than five seconds at a time, and the result for the public is often stultifying boredom. When in 1992 the Wimbledon men's championship was won by Andre Agassi, the result was especially welcomed by some critics, and the public at large, because Agassi's opponent, Goran Ivanisevic, had hardly done more than serve fast through the entire tournament (he had in fact served a record number of 206 clean aces, including 37 in the final). Similar public rejoicing was heard after Agassi's victories in the 1994 New York open championship, and in the 1995 Australian open in Melbourne. Agassi, whose game is about subtlety rather than strength, is the exception in the contemporary game. Ticket sales for that particular New York championship were at their lowest for over twenty years; many former tennis fans admitted to being bored with the game as currently played. It has been seriously suggested that the rules of the game will have to be changed in order to make men's tennis more entertaining, or public interest in the game (and therefore the interest of sponsors such as Volvo) will cease. One radical idea is the abolition of the second serve – if the first service had to be in play, fewer men would practise for service strength at the expense of the delicacy and creativity of touch which winners of the recent past like Connors and McEnroe displayed in abundance. The technology of the ball could also be to blame – another suggestion is to provide slower, more air resistant balls. An interim measure enacted in 1994 was that players should not pause for so long between serves.

So there are two areas of blame for boring male tennis. Much of the public debate on this question has implicitly indicted the male body; the players are too strong, it seems, to play 'good' tennis. Another aspect of the debate concerns the technology, the equipment which the players use. Balls fly faster through the air, and rackets are bigger and strung at a higher pressure so that they can hit the ball harder. While it has been suggested that the technology should be altered in order to make the game slower, and that the rules should be changed, no-one has yet suggested that male training routines should be altered in order to change the players' body language and give it more subtle accents.

There are similar problems at present in golf. The successful players of even the recent past were able to impart a delicacy of touch to the ball on the fairways or the green, or from the bunker, making the ball spin or fade to change direction, which more than made up for a lack of brute strength. Now, however, many young, and successful, players try to do two things only: hit the ball hard, and hit it straight. The debate here again is not only about the strength of the player: the technology of golf equipment has come under scrutiny. Clubs are now being manufactured from a variety of high-technology materials; the clubs known traditionally as 'woods' are now more often complex metal alloys, though carbon fibres and porcelain have also been used. As with tennis, the technology of the ball has also been improved. Computer aided, wind-tunnel assisted design has made balls which fly more consistently over longer distances, and also spin consistently. The current golf ball can make the amateur into a far better performer; but although it also makes the professional golfers more efficient, some of them regret the arrival of the new technologies. For them, it takes away some of the subtlety and individuality they were able to bring to bear on the game. Here, as in tennis, there are also contests between manufacturers, who sponsor players to use their equipment: the player with the best equipment has an advantage many see as unfair. Again there have been suggestions that championship tournaments should be equalised, in Guttmann's sense of equality of conditions for competition, with all players being given the same type of ball and club.

Many sports people feel that they are now less important than the equipment they use. Many members of the public and supporters likewise feel that they are being treated to displays of physical strength, or technological excellence, rather than contests in which the skill, subtlety and thought of the player are at stake. The final chapter will comment on the ideas of the pleasures of sport which are implicitly raised in these debates. Here the discussion will concentrate on aspects of the strength versus skill debate: the question of the body, and technology.

The first point is that this is not a binary opposition. The barriers between the body and technology are by no means clear. There are some sports, of course, in which there remains a clear distinction: it is easy to see that the players either are or are not distinguished because of superior equipment. The obvious example of the primacy of technology is in motorsports, pre-eminently formula one motor-racing. The grand prix racing driver may well be, indeed must be, a highly skilled operator. Grand prix machines are massive concentrations of high technology which demand a special kind of response from the driver, over and above the 'point and squirt' mentality of aggressive drivers in everyday life, or indeed everyday motor racing. In 1993 the driver Michael Andretti, with a successful record in Indy-car racing, failed as a grand prix driver for the McLaren team because he could not come to terms with the sophistication of the machinery (while in the same season formula one world champion Nigel Mansell, who had moved in the other direction, won the Indy-car championship with ease). However, driving skill is no longer the principal determinant of success, which depends almost entirely on the car. The cars with the most advanced and expensive engines, suspensions and body design are so much faster than the norm that they win – not every single race, but repeatedly: whoever is driving the best car becomes the world champion. This has the paradoxical, if obvious, effect of attracting the best drivers to the best cars; but drivers, however talented, who do not drive good cars do not win – in the recent past the Brazilian driver Emerson Fittipaldi, who had been successful for Lotus and Ferrari, insisted on driving machines of Brazilian design, and failed to win another race.

The real contest in formula one grand prix racing, then, is between teams of car designers and builders. This constructors' championship seems to so many people to be a negation of the meaning of sport that FISA, the governing body of grand prix racing, has repeatedly tried to curb or ban various technological developments, claiming that this is in an attempt to equalise the competition, and to make the sport less expensive. Lotus founder Colin Chapman fought a constant battle with

FISA over innovations (especially in suspension design) which made his cars unacceptably faster than the norm. Turbo-charged engines have recently been banned; at the time of writing it was proposed once again to ban certain technologies like computer-controlled 'active' suspension. As in tennis and golf, there are increasing pressures to move grand prix racing back to a contest primarily among drivers – in this case towards something like the American Indy-car racing system, in which the specifications for the design of the car are so rigidly controlled that all the cars are very similar, and because the engines are so powerful, chassis and suspension design is anyway less crucial in giving drivers the edge: in this case, the contest is much more between drivers than between machines.

The grand prix car is an example of the complex relationship between capital, design and performance. Over the years money has been invested in all aspects of car design. Car bodies have been made more aerodynamic, stronger and safer. Engines have been made more powerful, suspensions more immediately and infinitely adjustable, gearboxes more flexible (and recently semi-automatic, under the driver's direct control but without the bother of a clutch), tyres better suited to specific weather and road conditions. Almost everything in a car is now controlled by specially designed microcircuitry. Capitalism, as a system which seeks profit, has not benefitted straightforwardly from this, however. Desire for success, albeit fuelled by capital, has produced losses for many investors. The business of grand prix car design and construction has become so awesomely expensive that massive sponsorship is necessary for a team to have any chance of success; even major manufacturers like BMW, Honda and Renault have dipped in and out of grand prix racing, retiring because of the costs, despite the prestige of victory in the world's second best loved sport (after soccer, more people worldwide watch grand prix racing than any other sport), and then in Renault and Honda's case returning, because of the perceived kickbacks from grand prix success in sales of their more ordinary road cars.

While the grand prix driver is not an outstanding example of design for performance, drivers' bodies are in effect redesigned for their own safety: they are very valuable commodities. Drivers get to the top through a mixture of determination and wealth. They are fit and healthy; they are rewarded for their success with enormous sums of money, for which they risk their lives in public. But the risks are reduced not just by the design of the car (grand prix cars, made from composites based on carbon fibre technology, are much safer to crash than the average saloon) but through their high technology flame-retardant outfits; their heads are protected by hi-tech helmets, their eyes by hi-tech visors. The body of the driver, like the car, is constantly redesigned, in this case through the technology of sports clothing. Despite the deaths during the 1994 season, including that of the outstanding driver Ayrton Senna, given the speeds at which the cars are driven, grand prix racing has an outstanding safety record because of this redesign of the car and the body.

Everywhere in professional sport specific clothing is now a matter of supreme importance. At one level clothing is crucial to the success of the performer. Ski pants and cycling helmets are designed to increase airspeed through diminished wind resistance. Shoes are made for grip and spring. Studs on shoes are made for gripping contact with any kind of surface, both grass and artificial, and in any kind of weather. Gloves are made for minimum air resistance, for maximum contact with stick or ball, or both. Like the more obvious aspects of kit design – balls, clubs, rackets, skis and so on – sports clothing is designed to make the task of the player easier. Clothes are designed for success (and, again, safety) through redesigning the body.

There is no doubt that in many cases the redesign of the body which is offered by leading manufacturers can help to improve the performance of a leading athlete. There is equally no doubt that no manufacturer would develop a range of sports goods simply so that they could be worn by a few dozen wealthy and successful professionals. Sports equipment sales in Britain were worth over £2 billion in the early 1990s. Sports goods fulfil one or both of two functions: they help the amateur to play to a high standard, and help those who cannot even hit a ball to identify with the player or team of their choice. If there are leading edge products like grand prix tyres, for example, which are not suitable or available for road use, then the manufacturers will kindly supply a less specialised item with which the grand prix fan can identify – Goodyear sold a range of tyres under the 'grand prix' title. Sports goods are very big business; the body of the public performer is a clothes horse to advertise this business through success. In the case of casual clothing, sweat shirts, trainers and the like, this may make no difference to the performer (though it has made an enormous difference to fashion and everyday clothing). In some cases, though, it is safe to assume that the athlete who wears a specific brand of shoes might be more successful, but less wealthy, were she or he to switch to another brand. It has been claimed that a long-term sponsorship deal from a racket manufacturer helped to make tennis star Jimmy Connors a very wealthy man, but also denied him some championship winnings because the racket simply wasn't as good as some other available makes. Former basketball star Michael Jordan, on the other hand, claims that he helps to design, and approves of, all the sports goods he personally endorses – he wore his own-design, Nike-marketed, footwear on court, and won in it more consistently than any player in the history of the game. Golfers Jack Nicklaus, Gary Player and Arnold Palmer have gone one better and moved into the very lucrative business of designing and building golf courses: their expertise and renown as players enables them to charge considerably more than other golf course architects.

One form of contact between the public and the performers they idolise, then, is a form of consumerism which involves the purchase and wearing of the goods they endorse – or perhaps playing on the courses they have built. This exploitation of both public and performer is crucial to the success of the sports goods business and the teams and individuals they supply, and goods manufacturers like Adidas and Nike have risen on the backs of deals with performers and the successful marketing of products associated with success in sport. The desire of the fan to become part of the success of the team, and his or her willingness to spend money to symbolise that desire, leads to a short-term fashion cycle of team-based sports clothing. Team clothing is redesigned as soon as market researchers allow, in order that the devoted follower can buy another new strip (and preferably one each for the spouse and children as well) – and thus pay both the manufacturer, and a commission to the team and/or its owners.

The massive earnings available to the top performers over and above their already massive salaries are because of the very lucrative deals they can strike to endorse goods like shoes, shirts and sunglasses. Again, the effects of this on their identities are complex. The imagined community can still exist if everyone is wearing the same shirt, with the same player's name on it, but for the person whose existence the shirt is commemorating, to be the focus of that fan community through what is principally a commercial transaction symbolises the burden of expectation through which the sports champion must live, and which includes as its obverse the possibility of failure and scapegoating. The team shirt is, in other words, a symbol of the player's place in a capitalist system of exchange based on a fantasy about that player's body. For that lionised player then to change clubs, shirts, and so on, must at least disrupt the very important psychic drive for success, the desire-fantasy which is necessary for success as a representative. This is one reason why small club stars often fail when transferred to bigger clubs.

Fans often complain that too many players are mercenaries and do not give their all for the teams they play for. Debate current at the time of writing about the performance of English national cricket and football teams seems, oddly, to miss this question.[1] I argue that even at national level this primary form of identified motivation is missing from players whose careers are now principally mediated through desires for wealth rather than national and local identities. Without this loyalty, the temptation is always to move on, to earn another transfer fee, to run in another exhibition race . . . or to allow another manufacturer to sign up for a sponsorship deal which effectively redesigns the athlete's body, externally at least.

As the subject of capital development and technological experiment, the athlete is also prey to another common temptation: to redesign the body internally. At present this principally means recourse to drugs, both legal and illegal. The 'problem' of drugtaking in top competitive sport goes back at least a hundred years. Cyclists in the endurance contests which emerged as the forerunner of the Tour de France were known to take a fairly lethal-sounding mixture of strychnine, alcohol and caffeine; if that didn't give the required explosive performance, some cyclists added nitro-glycerine to the mixture.[2] This connection between cycling and drug-taking continues. One of the few outstanding British tour cyclists, Tommy Simpson, died after excessive use of performance-boosting drugs during the 1967 Tour de France.

But the internal redesign of the body can be achieved by other means than the crude resort to chemicals. Since World War Two, the number of techniques available for performance enhancement has increased rapidly. Not all involve drugs. Training at high altitude makes the body work harder to compensate for the lower air density and oxygen levels; moving to lower altitude for the actual competition then allows the player a few weeks' advantage before the body reverts to its normal pattern of work in standard atmospheric pressure. Blood doping (taking blood from the body, storing it, and then re-injecting the red cells at the last minute) increases the red cell count, and therefore the body's ability to process oxygen. Diet can be adjusted to promote stamina, short-term energy release, or the growth of strength and muscle bulk.

Then there are the illegal drugs, the current demon of the language of sport. Of the better known drugs, steroids increase muscle bulk, amphetamines increase stamina and aggression, and relaxants like beta blockers, alcohol and cannabis calm the nerves (important in precision activities like shooting). Some people take growth hormones to increase strength; female gymnasts may also take endocrine suppressants to delay the onset of puberty. All these substances affect the behaviour of the body and also the performer's mind-set; they make people feel calm, or increase their feeling of well-being, or heighten these positive feelings into 'improved' levels of aggression: the 'steroid rage' of American footballers being a well-known condition which presumably improves performance in a very aggressive sport. All these substances are addictive, and all are pleasurable; many people, apparently, like getting stoned on steroids, and take them for immediate personal pleasure as well as the longer-term physical benefits.

To some people, all this is quite simply cheating, and should be stopped. Attempts – fairly desultory attempts – have been made to 'clean' international athletics contests and other sports, through random drugtesting. Taking drugs, it is argued, contravenes the spirit of honest competition and fair play which was part of the British-influenced world sporting network, and which Baron De Coubertin enshrined in his Olympic Charter. It is, according to this argument, as wrong to take illegal drugs as it is to push over an opponent during a race, or to tackle in order to injure an opponent in the first minutes of a match, in the hope that the referee will not take action.

Apparently there is a straightforward moral argument here. Drugtaking is cheating, which is wrong. But even taking the argument at face value, there is an enormous problem: that of detection and punishment. Most athletes know when they are likely to be tested, and so can train until the last minute on drugs, allowing enough time for the traces to be washed through the system, while still benefitting from the stamina or muscle growth which the drugs have given them; or they can take substances which will mask the traces of the banned drugs, and carry on regardless. Many athletes will similarly take any new drug offered them on the basis that this will probably be undetectable, and even if it is discovered, will not be on a list of banned substances when they next compete. Those athletes who are discovered are not usually banned for life, and some are allowed to escape unpunished. There are many stories of positive tests being quietly lost, and of national committees rushing to defend their performers.

It is generally agreed that random testing at competition times does no more than scratch the surface of a problem which exists at all levels of the world of sport. It is not just a problem of the top level professional competitors. As with the design of sports equipment, the international illegal drugs industry would not be interested in supplying a few hundred athletes; the professional users are copied by those who wish to emulate them or to identify with them and their success. Amateur body-builders in health clubs all over the world are taking steroids in order to increase the size of their muscles; health clubs are therefore one hub of the illegal drugs trade. Drugs of all sorts are freely available. People of all sorts take them, for athletic as well as recreational purposes. As with the sports goods industry, the drug industry is a massive worldwide operation, in this case involving legal, semi-legal and illegal substances. The illegal drugs trade is said to have the second largest turnover (after arms sales) of any world business. To combat this global operation, many nation states operate customs and excise schemes, inspecting cars at borders, or raiding a few clubs now and then. Other nation states make a great show of suppressing manufacture. None suppress demand, or have tried to, or could. As with recreational drugs, so with drugs for sports performance. Where there is demand, there will be a supply.

The Faust Effect

But why the demand? The desire for drugs in sport works on two levels. At one, arguably the more important, there is the craving for success – what we might call the Faust effect. Many performers would cheerfully sell their souls to the devil in return for guaranteed success. Sports-players fantasise about success; they desire it; they wish to win, whatever the cost – boxers know of the dangers of brain damage, but box nonetheless; the Isle of Man TT motorcycle races continue to attract entrants, despite the annual toll of deaths and serious injuries. Tom Donohoe and Neil Johnson, in *Foul Play*, their book about drug-taking in sport, report an American survey which asked over one hundred athletes if they would take a drug which would guarantee success in the next championship, even if side effects might well include death within a year. Nearly 55 per cent said yes.[3] This fantasised narrative drives their being – as it does those of many other athletes on a local level, and their followers.

More generally, we live in an addictive culture. Drugs provide intensely pleasurable experiences for most of their users. Drugtaking is characterised as morally wrong by many groups of people. None have succeeded in abolishing the craving people have for drugs and their pleasures (one national attempt to do so, the 1919–33 prohibition of alcohol sales in the United States of America, only resulted in a massive increase in the power and influence of organised crime). The combination of the general wish for chemical redesign with the specific desire for athletic success is irresistible.

Another aspect of this argument must be confronted. The position that equates drug use with cheating has a lot going for it. It may well confer unfair advantage. But so do sport-specific training facilities and time for training; advanced diets; sessions with sports psychologists; and special clothing and equipment. The grand prix car designed best wins the championship. Similarly, the America's Cup yacht race has for several years been a confrontation between technologies (and the funds needed to design and build technologically innovative boats) rather than crews. When cyclist Chris Boardman broke several records on his way to Olympic success at Barcelona in 1992, he used a bicycle of a revolutionary new design, developed by the Lotus car company, which he first showed in public at the Olympics – to stop anyone else developing a similar machine. Boardman's greatest rival since then, on the other hand, has been Graham Obree, an obsessive Scot who has built his own bike from a few bits of scrapyard piping. The cycling bureaucracy has made great efforts since to stop Obree from competing at major events, because his success with a self-made bike would endanger the lucrative tie-up between major investment and sporting success. All machines not routinely available could be said to confer unfair advantage on the player; all are aspects of design technology (even where the designer is a hobbyist amateur like Obree). So are performance enhancing drugs. Why, then, is there so much more opposition to the internal redesign of the athlete's body than the external?

The problem seems to be that the human body, a collection of bones and orifices and connecting tissue, has somehow disappeared into that dangerous territory, 'common sense'. It has become naturalised, taken for granted as an authentic, and to many people sacred, entity whose composition is fixed and cannot, or rather should not, be altered. The body has arguably become the last site of humanism; in his arguments about the voice, which I shall discuss in Chapter Six, even the structuralist Roland Barthes seems to argue for an essential, centred authenticity to the body. Morally and politically there may be something in this argument: morality sets up belief systems with which we can understand the world and our place in it, and therefore act. The belief that there is an essential, unalterable truth about the human body is comforting and empowering (we act in the world in the belief that we are physically and mentally stable enough to do so). Biologically, however, it is nonsense. Bodies are a hive of constantly changing and interchanging chemical and neurological information; under stress, the body naturally produces many substances whose effects are similar to those of drugs such as amphetamines and opiates. Different bodies exposed to similar conditions will react differently, and alter their chemical composition (and therefore their ability to perform athletically) differently.

Taken as a whole, human bodies can be characterised; in particular, they are distinct, and individualised. Even the chemical composition of the body is not an invariant, and it is not usefully quantifiable, even in what might seem a promising area of distinction, the difference between men and women. Fears that men could successfully compete as women led to sex tests for women athletes, which in the early days relied on voyeuristic examination, and latterly have also involved complex chemical analyses. Several successful female competitors have been 'revealed' as 'men' on their deaths – though this in itself can be a fairly hazy definition based on external appearance. But strange as it may seem, there are in fact no reliable sex tests based on hormone levels or chromosome patterns.[4] The chemical evidence in sex testing has revealed that endocrine tests can 'prove' masculinity in the case of people with breasts and ovaries, and femininity in the case of people who have penises and testicles. Sport does not, and in the case of competitive sport is not supposed to, equalise these 'natural' biochemical differences. Drugs are an aspect of the design for performance which cannot be successfully controlled. The only morally acceptable policy, therefore, should be to make them as freely and openly available as possible to athletes as to everyone else, to list their potential dangers, and police their use through rigorous and constant testing. Drug use in sport should at least be tolerated and if necessary its side effects treated. It cannot be banned.

The body and mind of the player are in almost all sports the centre of attention; even in grand prix racing the personalities of drivers like Ayrton Senna and Nelson Piquet are given more media attention than the exquisite machinery they are paid to operate. But the sporting mind/body is not a fixed entity; as well as being the subject of redesign by sports clothing manufacturers, and the constant flux of its biochemistry, it is obviously subject to constant repetitive stress and to injury. Either can threaten careers. Psychological stress caused the early retirement of two of the best known and most talented British footballers of the 1960s, Jimmy Greaves and George Best. Injuries through bad tackles have more often meant early retirement for footballers, for example, in the 1980s, Danny Thomas and Gary Stevens. But many players are being laid low by injuries sustained through routine training and performance. Most athletes may in fact be too physically fit for their own good. Recent scientific work has suggested that constant training for the peak of fitness can leave the body more open to viral infections, leading to collapse during competition, or at worst to early retirement from sporting competition: this is especially a problem for young players whose bodies are overstressed before their physical peak is possible. Tennis player Tracey Austin, for example, won tournaments in her teens but had to retire before her twenty-first birthday. It is not only young performers who suffer in this way. English middle-distance runner Sebastian Coe blamed poor performance at one Olympic meeting on over training. Similarly, overtraining has been blamed for the failure of some race horses, whose capillary systems rupture, causing bleeding in the lungs during races. Many athletes, like many professional dancers, find that overtraining and performing through slight injury means that they are virtually crippled in retirement: arthritis is common. Drugs taken to enhance performance or control pain can also have painful or even dangerously toxic long-term side effects. Footballer Diego Maradonna has several times had operations to remove cortisone from his knees. The cortisone had been injected as a painkiller; large doses build up and begin to calcify, thus worsening the knee's physiological problems: painkillers can enable athletes to perform through injury, but this will usually worsen the long-term effects of those injuries.

Where does all this chemical redesign leave the body? Despite the increasing presence of chemical and physical aids to sports performance, at present it is beginning to appear that an end is in sight to the constant and astonishing rollback of record times and weights which have so far characterised the century of modern competitive sport. The pace of change in most men's events has slowed dramatically: new records are set in tenths of a second in many events. Women's performances, as I noted in Chapter Two, are on a faster upward curve, presumably because women have been competing as professional athletes for a far shorter time. The astonishing performance by Chinese women runners in the 1993 Asian athletics championships underlines the prediction that in some events such as middle- and long-distance running they will overtake men early in the next century (though it is noteworthy that the immediate reaction of the opponents of these women was to accuse them of taking drugs, and subsequent investigations into their coaching methods and diets have led to controversy over the role of their coach).

But apart from the Chinese record breakers, even women are not pushing back the barriers as they were: the performance curve is beginning to flatten. The strength and malleability of the body must have finite limits, whatever the resources of equipment, training, sports psychology and drugs: in the case of the male body in particular it may be close to those limits. In the case of horse racing, the biological limit may already have been reached. Racehorses, almost all of which are genetically derived from half a dozen Arab horses imported into England in the eighteenth century, have been running at comparable times for fifty years: some individuals are faster than others, but none are setting new speed records. It seems that the limits of the human (or equine) body will at some point prevent the further pushing back of athletic performance barriers.

But this may be an oversimplification. There is one way in which the body of the sports competitor could be and probably will be remade. One very strong recent public fantasy indicates the ways in which people may wish to move towards athletic success: this is the model of the heroic male body which emerged in Arnold Schwarzenegger's film about body-building, *Pumping Iron* (1977). Hollywood has since adopted this body-type as the norm for its individual, interventionist heroic masculinity, with stardom for Jean Claude Van Damme (and a more worked-out Sylvester Stallone) among the results. Perhaps predictably, it has not allowed the developed female body the same space – the sequel *Pumping Iron II – the Women* (1979) was itself ambivalent about female bodybuilding; massive muscularity has, it seems, to be seen as the property of manhood. In many films, notoriously the two *Terminator* films, both starring Schwarzenegger, this body is further perfected by being robotised. The invincible human being, the Superman for our times, is apparently a cyborg. This may seem a long way removed from the local judo champion or the national winner over 100 metres, whose humanity is obvious in that they are fallible: they lose as well as win. However mechanically he played, Bjorn Borg eventually lost a Wimbledon final – to John McEnroe, a far less routinised performer. But in some ways a future of competition between cyborgs is a strong possibility.

The Frankenstein Effect?

Stories are already told of athletes whose bodies have so much metal in them, plates and screws holding together broken bones, kneecaps and so on, that they are stopped by airport metal detectors. Footballer Paul Gascoigne's knee became an object of national concern in 1991; a film was made of the surgical repair of the knee, which now permanently incorporates a few pieces of metal. As well as the redesign of the soft parts of the machine, through drugs which increase muscle bulk or retard puberty, there are many performers whose hard physical material has been extensively redesigned in this way, through surgery after injury, but who continue to compete at the highest level. The possibilities exist here for 'cheating'. Orthopaedic surgery has often advanced through the treatment of sporting injuries. Surgeons have developed expertise in the repair of bone and cartilage to the extent that joints can be replaced and whole limbs can be reconstructed: plastic and metal hips are routinely inserted into the bodies of elderly people. Surgeons are beginning to use 'myoelectric prostheses', replacement limbs with small electric motors, linked to existing muscle and nerves.[5] Though these are currently at the experimental stage, and do not work as well as conventional arms and hands, it is to be expected that they will become routine within a generation, in the same way that some forms of replacement or repair surgery (such as kidney transplants or heart bypass operations) have become routine. In a world in which health care is becoming commercialised and commodified, it is to be expected that bodily improvement mechanisms will be made generally available.

The aesthetic redesign of the body is already routine. Cosmetic surgery is now widespread in the wealthy parts of the world. Men and women queue up to have their bodies reshaped in the name of beauty; fat is removed, breasts and pectoral muscles enlarged or diminished, hair transplanted and so on. Recent legislation in the USA has questioned the use of silicon as an implant; it may have some tendency to harden, or the bags containing the material to burst, with unfortunate effects for the person into whose body the material has been sown. But silicon is passive (as is some peoples' idea of beauty). Implants could just as easily be active, helping the shape of the body in movement as well as at rest. Many people are already kept alive through implanted microprocessors – the heart pacemaker. Current pacemakers are not just battery operated clocks, as the first generation of crude machines were; they are programmable devices, *linked into the body's nervous system*, which respond to its electrical impulses with their own electric signals. They can be reprogrammed from outside the body without the need for further operations. A runner could, potentially, set her or his own pacemaker differently for sprints or middle-distance races; or control it using a remote control.

This may seem far-fetched. Medicine has always been about repair, restoration. Heart pacemakers are at present given to those whose hearts are failing. But the example of cosmetic surgery shows that medical technologies can be used to improve the lives of the well. There is no reason why implanted microprocessors should not for instance release drugs into the system when neurologically stimulated, or help to control the muscles during throwing or running, or even in combination with a series of motors replace that most ridiculous aspect of the human body, the knee. The animatronics used in the creation of Hollywood special effects creatures such as the dinosaurs of Spielberg's *Jurassic Park* could, if combined with human aptitudes like unprogrammed 'instinctive' response, presumably help the body to transcend the limits imposed by evolution – including the knee. The new orthopaedic techniques mentioned above will be an important part of this process and of the rethinking of the human body which will accompany it. One way to improve sports performance in the future may be closer to cyberpunk fiction than current 'sports science'.

Another potential development is provided by the project, now under way, to decode human DNA – the set of biochemical instructions which are present in every cell of our bodies, and which control physical development. The mapping of all this information, the 'human genome', is currently on course for completion around the turn of the century. When completed it will offer another possibility in the genetic manipulation of the human body before birth. The headline version of this revolves around the idea, common in science fiction, of 'cloning', the exact reproduction of life forms through the use of DNA rather than the more hit-and-miss efforts of sexual reproduction (as in the rather far-fetched example of *Jurassic Park*).

Athletes could be 'cloned', at least in the sense that the genetic information provided by the parents could be optimised to produce children with spectacular possibilities for physical development. (Some athletes might wish to make money by donating sperm, eggs, or their own DNA). Genetic technologies are intellectual property, their patents the property of biotechnological companies, so this kind of treatment is unlikely to become universally available. For those with the money, a brave new world awaits in which it will be perfectly possible to produce children to order. But would all the right physical equipment necessarily make them world-beating shot-putters or long-distance cyclists?

Here we have to return to the mind-set of the athlete. Sports science is, necessarily, complemented by sports psychology. Professional coaches are often aided and abetted by psychologists who spend time with their clients trying to persuade them to think positively: that they are in command, that their opponents are poor, that they can repeat previous performances and/or cut out mistakes – that they will win. Throughout this book it has been argued that the desires and fantasies of the performer and public are necessary for sport to have any meaning for us. Now it could be that the genetically engineered, cybernetically assisted sportsperson of the future will also have a mind connected to or even controlled by microprocessor circuits – in which case the desire to succeed, and the terms in which that success is envisioned (national pride, fame, wealth or whatever), might be programmed in along with the desire to be nice to the coach, to get up early and do a ten mile run before breakfast, or to smile when signing autographs for the fan. Such mental programming, as well as the physical restructuring, may be claimed to cross the line between what is authentically human and what is robotic; in which case we are back to the terms in which opponents of drug use see the authentically human.

This is not a very impressive argument; though, as I have said, even Roland Barthes sometimes writes as if the authentically human is the body, in the end it usually relies on the suggestion that our bodies and capacities have been given us by God, and that we should not tamper with them. At the end of a century which has seen human beings murder millions of other human beings physically undistinguishable from themselves, through bombs, gas chambers, deliberate mass starvation, and so on, the reliance on a notion of human authenticity is not reassuring. Cybernetically assisted sportspeople would do less harm in a future world than non-cyborg communists and Nazis have done already, and may do again.

To approach the issue from another angle: 'Love is a Contact Sport', as the wonderful Whitney Houston has reminded her listeners.[6] One very important aspect of late twentieth century culture has been the athleticisation of sex. Since the publication of the work of Masters and Johnson, beginning with *Human Sexual Response* in 1966,[7] human sexual behaviour has been rationalised and medicalised, subject to a routinised language of gesture and procedure which was recognised by Weber as an aspect of modernisation in general, and by Guttmann as part of the modernisation of sport. In particular, through a system of electronic measurements on (volunteer) laboratory subjects, Masters and Johnson 'proved' that the female orgasm is the direct result of the stimulation of the clitoris. This was immediately reported, and used in feminist discourse and the salacious press alike, as 'The Myth of the Vaginal Orgasm', a topic of endless fascination and debate. Sexual response, then, was subject to the measurement of performance, and the language of training and preparation, performance, performance-enhancing equipment, even statistical approaches to the incidence of arousal and orgasm, became part of the languages of the erotic and of pornography. Through popular textbooks like Alex Comfort's *The Joy of Sex*, and subsequent gay and lesbian equivalents (including recent CD-ROM versions), human sexuality became both considered, and practised, as an aspect of athletics, of rationalised, quantifiable performance.

Sport has always been the site of sexual fantasy – often rather damagingly, as in the film *Best Practice*, which stereotypes female athletes as lesbians, 'other' to 'normal' womanhood. But it is increasingly possible through sport's ability to reshape and rethink the body, to imagine a future of new sexual differences and desires in which that 'normal' is no longer available. Aldous Huxley, one man who saw the future more clearly than most, imagined in his great novel *Brave New World* (1932) a sexuality based on the idea of play rather than the limits of biology; if he could not move beyond some of the accepted specifics of gender and sexual preference, we can; and probably will. The whole question of physical authenticity – even the question of stable physical personality, a body stable enough to produce narcissism – would cease to operate; and a good thing too, perhaps, for those of us who spend most of our time exercising our muscles or our appetite-control in order to achieve an impossible shape. But ... good, with the usual caveat. Technological solutions to the limits of the body are on the whole First World solutions. A brave new world in which sporting and sexual personae are mutable only when and for whom the price is right will be an even more dangerous and divided world than the current rather troubled entity.

Nevertheless, it is worth thinking about the advantages of these potential transformations. In a very influential article first published in 1985, Donna Haraway argued the advantages of her 'Manifesto for Cyborgs'; this manifesto was a specifically feminist intervention in the envisioning of the technologies of the future.[8] Haraway argued that the idea of the cyborg, an intelligent machine, was potentially liberating to women. There was no reason why a feminised machine should not stand for a future in which women have overcome the damaging mind/body split, and its construction in favour of men. We have seen in recent years how the internet has allowed an electronic masquerade, including the possibility of electronic transsexuality: users can choose their own gendered identity *as users*, and inhabit that gender while logged on, another when logged off the net. Cyborg feminism promises to undermine the stability of gender relations altogether by proposing a new set of relationships between the body and intelligence. Haraway opposed this idea to the radical feminist essentialism of a writer like Mary Daly, who saw the increasing technological interference with childbirth as a patriarchal device to control women through science – and perhaps render them obsolete altogether. Such writing tends to equate 'woman' with a set of biological particulars, focused on motherhood. For Haraway, this reference back to the magic of fertility can only at best perpetuate gender divisions, and since the point for her is not to describe but to change or abolish them, she wrote, 'I would rather be a cyborg than a goddess'.

One of the problems with Haraway's work, and with interpretations of it, is that it tends to see these relationships in terms of metaphor – it is about ways of seeing the body and intelligence – whereas radical critiques of medical technology, such as Daly's, are about real physical transformations of the body and their potential. Let us rework sport into the tapestry, as an aspect of fantasy but also as a set of real physical practices. As both practice and fantasy, sport is one of the ways in which men are naturalised *not* as male culture versus female nature, or male rationality as opposed to female emotionality, or male mind versus female body, but as physical entities. Sport is one of the few ways in which the male body is continually represented, examined, worshipped: all too often to the exclusion of the female body-as-active. A sporting future in which the bodies of both men and women can be reworked technologically, and their potentials equalised, will demonstrate in precisely the ways in which Haraway predicts, that gender has no fixed boundaries of physicality; it will undermine those essential stabilities, and will provide a physical platform for the overcoming of the assumed limits of sexed identity. Trans-sexual modifications of the athlete's body (such as in the case of the tennis player Renée Richards) are a crude enough starting point; the medical potential already exists for a future in which sporting participation knows no gendered limits, and someone born a girl, who wants to play professional men's football, can do so. You hesitate? Body-builders and weightlifters, in order to succeed, routinely take drugs which drastically alter the physical structure and chemical composition of their bodies. There is no reason why other athletes should not equally routinely resort to structural alteration, biochemical or microprocessor-based implants or the like; if that blurs the existing gender divisions, well fine.

Design, Performance and the Public

What are the implications for the public world of sport of an increasingly cybernetic sporting élite, reliant for competitive success on the external design technologies of sports clothing and machinery, and internally on the artificial reconstructions of minds and bodies produced by drugs, genetic programming, microsurgery and even microcircuitry?

Clearly if this process proceeds so far as to divorce the performer altogether from the general human characteristics described above, then sport will have entered a new phase, and the definition offered at the start of the book would have to be rewritten entirely. One of the things we take for granted about sport is that it involves humans competing against each other. Already, however, there are a few alternatives to this model – sports in which non-human representatives compete. In pursuits such as pigeon racing and greyhound racing (and illegal dog fights and other animal confrontations) direct human competition is mediated through the animals, though even here the input of humans as owners, trainers and bureaucratic organisers, and in the case of greyhound racing and dog fights as spectators, remains significant. If there is to be a future in which human-based cyborgs, or even robots worked into a parody of the human form, compete, then we can assume that computer-aided designers will be inputting to the final outcome. If this future for professional sport begins to sound a little too much like the world of computer games, then we can console ourselves with the reflection that *we* will still be able to go for a swim or pop down the road for a round of golf – perhaps with the stimulating accompaniment of performance-enhancing drugs: a coffee or two, or even, on the golf course, a whisky-filled hip flask.

It is also perfectly possible that continuing innovations in computer technology will render the role of the professional sports performer obsolete, in the wealthy West and Pacific Rim at least. Arcade games based around the skills of driving, flying, the martial arts, team sports like soccer and individual sports like golf are already popular. Computers will here transform the potentialities of the body, as they have in other fields. Two common examples: through the use of computer software, people without good brush technique can paint, and people without the ability to play musical instruments can compose and perform music. The growth of 'virtual reality' games, in their infancy at present, will enable those without the physical attributes of the successful athlete, but with a certain amount of mental dexterity, to experience the pleasures of the sporting contest without the years of training and self-discipline required for 'real' performance – and without the need for the construction of the facilities needed for mass participation.

This could help to solve a pressing social and ecological problem. In overcrowded Japan, sports facilities are expensive. Golf courses cannot be built in or around towns or cities because of the protection given to agricultural land; those that have been built recently are in mountainous terrain, requiring chairlifts between holes in many instances; the clubs which provide these facilities are prohibitively expensive, with annual subscriptions running into millions of dollars per person. One 'solution' to the problem has been for wealthy, but not super-wealthy Japanese to form consortia to buy land in other countries all over the world, build courses on this land, and fly to play even a weekend's golf in places as far away as Britain. This simply transplants, and multiplies, the vast ecological problems of the golf course. Which are: firstly, that in many people's eyes they disfigure the landscape; secondly, that they restrict its leisure use to subscribers or members; thirdly, that they use far too much water, at the expense of local people and their agriculture; in poorer countries they have even displaced whole settlements. New golfing complexes tend to have associated hotels and other leisure facilities, all of which bring tourists to areas where they are not wanted by most residents, and where the rest of the transport infrastructure cannot provide for them.

There is an ecological counter-argument. In Britain at least, agricultural land is also an ecological disaster, poisoned with fertiliser and denuded of trees and hedgerows, making food which is often a subsidised 'surplus'. Golf courses, which provide pleasant and easy contact with a tame and approachable landscape, interrupt these bleak semi-deserts, providing more trees and shrubs, and therefore sheltering far more insects, small mammals and birds than the barley fields of subsidised agribusiness. (Similar arguments can be made about fox-hunting. Paradoxically, hunting requires a certain amount of preservation; fox 'coverts', small areas of woodland, are another ecological bonus, especially in the otherwise arid English midlands. Hunting also preserves foxes themselves, which might otherwise be poisoned, trapped, shot or otherwise exterminated by the farmers who poison the land).

The demand for golf remains enormous. For the less wealthy Japanese (and increasingly for many people in Britain who cannot afford club fees or who cannot get onto waiting lists), large enclosed driving ranges are available, but overcrowded. Virtual golf will be able to provide the experience of golf without the spatial transformations needed by the 'real' thing. Virtual fishing, a slightly less complex programming exercise, is already highly successful in Japan.

Where do such innovations leave the body? This would no doubt depend on the way in which virtual technologies are developed. In some, there is a substitution of minimal gestures (the small-scale control of wrist or ankle movements) for the grand gestures of competitive sport – you could compare the different methods of acting for stage, with its big gestures, and television, with its concentration on close-ups and small gestures. But it does not have to be like this. It is perfectly possible to accommodate all the physical intensity of competition. A treadmill-based Virtual Marathon could well involve exactly the same physical stress as the 'real' thing; but an entire race could take place in one stadium, or for the city marathons, perhaps a local landmark like a park or a city square, with participants' running linked to screens replicating the route, and with treadmills which altered their gradient to match the programmed topography. The saving in traffic control and disruption would make this an attractive proposition. At any event, the sports centres whose technologies shape the bodies of their customers, promising fitness, firmness and physical control into middle age, could well offer them the ability to train at virtual sports. Through this process the distance between participant and public could be shortened yet further.

Does this sound far-fetched? It isn't. August 1994 saw the American launch of the Cybergear Virtual Reality exercise bicycle. A 25-inch high definition screen linked to a PC system with CD-ROM drive and soundcard provides changing images and sounds for the 'cyclist' who grips handlebars which pivot, turn, and gyrate in response to speed, direction and road conditions. Gearing and braking effects are provided; pedal resistance increases according to gearing and topography. The user can exercise at various levels of difficulty, or through networking can race against other people in the same room or exercise centre, or via the internet, against anyone with similar equipment anywhere else in the world.[9] Technology is changing the limits of the body, and of the imagined community, through the provision of virtual sport.

Notes

1. Partial exceptions are J. Walvin, *Football and the Decline of Britain*, Penguin, Harmondsworth, 1986; M. Marqusee, *Anyone but England: Cricket and the National Malaise*, Verso, London 1994.

2. Holt, *op.cit.*, p98.

3. T. Donohoe and N. Johnson, *Foul Play: Drug Abuse in Sports*, Blackwell, Oxford 1986, p125.

4. See F. Dyer, *Catching up the Men*, p66.

5. See for an overview R.N. Scott, 'Myoelectric Control Systems research at the Bioengineering Institute, University of New Brunswick', *Medical Progression Through Technology*, Volume 16, Number 1, May 1990, pp5-10. For discussions of prostheses in use, e.g. D.H. Silcox, M.D. Rooks, R.R. Vogel, and L.L. Fleming, 'Myoelectric Prostheses: A long-term follow-up and a study of the use of alternate prostheses', *Journal of Bone & Joint Surgery*, Volume 75, Number 12, December 1993, pp1781-9; J.M. Meredith and J.E. Vellendahl, 'Successful voluntary grasp and release using the cookie crusher myoelectric hand in 2-year olds', *American Journal of Occupational Therapy*, Volume 47, Number 9, September 1993, pp825-9; K. Bergman, L. Ornholmer, K. Zackrisson and M. Thyberg, 'Functional benefit of an adaptive myoelectric prosthetic hand compared to a conventional myoelectric hand', *Prosthetics and Orthotics International*, Volume 16, Number 1, April 1992, pp32-7.

6. Whitney Houston, 'Love is a Contact Sport', written by Preston Glass, from the album *Whitney*, Arista, 1987.

7. W.H. Masters and V.E. Johnson, *Human Sexual Response*, Little Brown, New York 1966.

8. D. Haraway, 'A Manifesto for Cyborgs: Science, Technology and Socialist Feminism in the 1980s', in L.J. Nicholson (ed), *Feminism/ Postmodernism*, Routledge, London 1990. A neat commentary is J. Halberstam, 'Automating Gender: Postmodern Feminism in the age of the Intelligent Machine', *Feminist Studies*, Volume 17, Number 3, Fall 1991, pp439-459. My thanks to Susan Worth for an illuminating discussion of this issue.

9. M. Hewitt, 'Getting on Your Virtual Bike', *The Independent*, June 3, 1994.

6 Presentation and Representation

Sport and Television

A transformation of the consumer into a virtual participant is already reshaping the public relationship with sporting activity, and to a certain extent changing physically active 'sports' into mentally active 'games'. The public presence in spectator sport may also change drastically because of technological changes in the way sport is consumed. Public sporting occasions are at present dominated by television, advertising and corporate sponsorship. Television fees mean that it effectively owns some sports. Ownership means control – and often quite drastic change. Worldwide coverage of sports has globalised games which had been seasonal: cricket, soccer and tennis are constantly available for the consumer of television sports. Television is increasingly able to design and redesign the structure of the contests it transmits, insisting on advertisement breaks, for example: American football matches are hours longer than actual playing time because of this requirement, although as yet crowds for the live spectacle seem unaffected. American television has put pressure on world soccer authorities to agree to changes in the structure of their game, asking for more breaks to make it more advertiser friendly, and for bigger goals to guarantee more goals, to make it more spectator friendly. Sponsors and other advertisers have changed the shapes of stadia, and the appearance of performers and their equipment, which are festooned with words and logos. Corporate sponsors have grabbed all the best seats inside stadia, but don't always sit in them, to the annoyance of potential spectators who cannot afford tickets; they are liable to be lunching during sessions of play. At venues from Wembley Stadium for soccer internationals to the riverside sites of the Henley Regatta, the annual English rowing festival, live sport has become the site of conspicuous consumption, in which sponsors display themselves and talk to their clients against the backdrop of the sporting event. As with prestige musical occasions, from opera to big-name rock concerts, the fan is all too often excluded either from the event altogether or from certain areas within the arena. The net effect of this process is to reassert the hold of television over live sport, even for the fans for whom its coverage is seen as banal; or technically inadequate; or both.

This dominance of the public presentation of the game by television and sponsorship means that despite sport's hold over television (as programming which delivers large audiences), television tries to structure sport within its confines, through constructing a specific type of knowledge of sport. With presenters and commentators, computer-assisted analysis, interviews with participant players and coaches, replays of controversial incidents, and so on, the game is redesigned by the television context, and this too changes its meaning for the public, whose expectations of the games they watch change because of this televised knowledge. Paying spectators were often heard a few years ago lamenting the absence of instant replay facilities from their seats; many stadia now have giant screens for that very purpose (and to carry yet more advertising between controversial incidents). In many ways the profusion of commentary and analysis is necessary because of the inadequacy of coverage. For many years the television directors sought to replicate the 'ringside view' of the spectator. In the case of boxing, and small-court sports like tennis, badminton or volleyball, the enclosed space of the contest is small enough for this to be possible: one camera can easily comprehend the whole playing area. But the coverage of most sports by the television cameras, for all the control this may offer the director, alters the spatial structures on offer to the spectator. The camera tends to follow the ball, on the reasonable assumption that that is where the action is. However, focusing on the ball or the players who hold the ball in team sports like soccer or rugby means that the spectator cannot see the geometry of opposition which is the crucial part of the contest: the 'running off the ball' by which the players of the better-prepared teams create space and scoring opportunities is usually invisible to the domestic spectator. Given current technology, the resolution offered by the television screen cannot accommodate the whole-pitch view that would enable the viewer to see these spatial relationships as they happen.

This lack is most obvious in the coverage of golf, in which it is routinely impossible to see the ball's flight in relation to the structure of the course. Similarly in squash, despite the smallness of the court, the ball is usually too fast for the (human-operated) camera: this most popular participant sport has therefore received hardly any television coverage, and the great deeds of the Pakistani family which has dominated men's squash, notably Jahangir Khan and Jansher Khan, have not been adequately recorded. In some cases, on the other hand, the use of very small cameras has offered the spectator excitements and privileged views which would not be possible without television, and which provide real insight. The stump camera in cricket matches, and the over-the-shoulder or helmet camera in grand prix racing and other motorsports, give a player's eye view of proceedings which, in not attempting to replicate the ringside seat, give a genuinely enhanced view of the game. All the less reason for the proliferation of commentary and analysis by experts, and all the more reason for a different kind of commentary on the pleasures of the game as televised.

The factual analysis and expertise offered in televised analysis is not the only way in which sport is and has been consumed, however. At one level this is a deeply objective way of seeing what is for most people a deeply subjective experience, revolving around the successes and failures of favourite teams and players, and the demonisation of particular opponents or referees. Most television commentary and analysis, with its statistical base and attempted neutrality, makes no attempt to replicate the emotional experience of sport. Thanks to the fan-led textual innovations discussed below, the televised coverage of soccer in England has begun to catch up with this very different viewpoint, that of the fan rather than the expert. Unfortunately coverage of other sports is still in the hands of expert commentators. At another level, however, that of the nation, the public, emotional world of the fan is routine for the commentators and analysts, whose objectivity disapears as the national colours are displayed. The nation and its sporting successes and failures are presented as an emotional entity, and the reaction to sporting failure is led by the television presentation thereof: it seems that experts have feelings too. This transformation of benevolent enthusiasm into unthinking chauvinism, of presenter into advocate, can be most disturbing; however, it continues to signal the importance of the media to the construction of the nation state, and the importance of sport in the continued presentation of the nation as an imagined community.

As was argued in Chapter Two, the relationships between the sporting event and the imagined community can be brought out far more clearly through a television presentation, and a far wider public addressed than the supporter or fan. However, there is no necessary connection between forms of broadcasting and political ideologies. Given the global structures and desires of capital, the question becomes important: will television wish to continue with this nationally-based presentation, or will televised sport shift perspective and become either continental or local? Will existing boundaries within Europe, for instance, keep televised sport and nation bound together, or will satellite technology mean that the 'best' in sport will be presented across national boundaries, using circus-style presentation and performance, and will therefore undermine national meanings? Will narratives of nation lose their power in the broadcast age of postmodernity?

For those who consider nationalism to be the worst

legacy of the nineteenth century, this potential technological conquest of nationalism might be welcome, whatever it does to the meaning of sports whose emergence was so bound up with the meaning of nation and empire. Television, however, has a way of accentuating the negative in its transforming practices.

Global formats like soaps and game shows also include the most anodyne forms of sports entertainment, most 'spectacularly' perhaps the produce of the World Wrestling Federation. In a ritualised parody of the circus version of sport, large men pretend to hurt each other. They pretend to assault the referee. They (genuinely) insult the crowd. There are personalities on show here, bodies to emulate, but no sense of local, regional or national community; no sense of narrative; none even of victory or defeat: winners and losers are clearly playing roles, and the results are as obvious in advance as at the most corrupt football or boxing match.

A related entertainment, involving women participators as well as men, is the 'Gladiators' series. Here, in a purpose-built studio, before a baying audience, a few well-built men and women with stage names like those of the professional wrestlers (Wolf, Hulk, etc) take on members of the public in contests of strength and skill (in that order). The Gladiators themselves tend to be professional sports performers – Kate Staples, a.k.a. Zodiac, is a leading female pole vaulter, who has pioneered women's pole vault as a contest in Britain. In a bizarre echo of the sporting world, in early 1995 Jefferson King, a.k.a. Shadow, was kicked off the show after testing positive for steroids. The tabloid press treats the gladiators themselves in the same way as the presenters of the show, as stars/champions/scapegoats; successful members of the public are famous for fifteen minutes, carnival kings and queens for a day. Public allegiance is to the show, or the channel – or not. Television has here not so much redesigned sport as effaced it, in the image of its most successful product, the game show.

Hollywood's acute parody-commentary on this event, *Running Man* (1991), is too close to the bone for comfort. Clearly, as the title implies, 'Gladiators' is derived from the Roman circus entertainment in which people would fight to the death. In *Running Man*, set in a future dominated by a global capitalism which maintains public loyalty through entertainment, criminals are released into a controlled environment, then hunted down and killed by professional gladiators. The film's hero (Arnold Schwarzenegger, this time not playing a cyborg), successfully combats the professional killers and takes the programme off the air.

Text/Discourse and Sport

Television presents sport within a set of its own values, and if in the case of programming like 'Gladiators' and world wrestling it offers a distorted version of what the rest of the world agrees to be sport, then its presentation of Olympic festivals or golf tournaments is still, necessarily, televisual. But television is not the only value structure which has, however symbiotically, changed the way sport works in our society. The presence of sport in news reports on radio and in newspapers underlines the point. Sport does not have a life of its own; it is not, and never has been, a region which develops autonomously outside all social contact. The rules governing sports are, of course, written in language, and therefore necessarily incorporate many of the common ideological codes of the societies in which they are written. As the final chapter will indicate, language does not dictate the whole meaning of sport, but through its rules, constantly polices its boundaries. Sport is both partly constructed within discourse, and itself a constant generator of discourse, from full-length books to pub chat.

There is not, then, a one-way relationship in which sport receives and expresses social codes. The language of sport is a constant source of analogy for other social situations. The sporting analogy is a constant presence in all kinds of text – as it has been for as long as people have been writing. Writing his letter to the Corinthians in the first century AD, St Paul said:

Know ye not that they which run in a race run all, but one receiveth the prize? So run, that ye may obtain. And every man that striveth for the mastery is temperate in all things. Now they do it to obtain a corruptible crown, but we an incorruptible. I therefore run, not as uncertainly; so fight I, not as one that beateth the air; but I keep under my body, and bring it into subjection.[1]

Already here we seem to be in the world of sport described by Robert Guttmann. The signs are all there: the striving for victory; the preparation of the body through 'temperate' self-discipline; the constant presence of desire (for the heavenly reward) which drives the body to maintain its discipline. Yet the passage remains an analogy, in which sporting discipline is used to describe the disciplines necessary to defy earthly temptation in order to achieve reward in heaven.

Sporting analogies are more constant in the discourse of warfare. Here is a passage from an English biography of the French military dictator and self-crowned Emperor Napoleon Bonaparte, published in 1939, the year of the outbreak of World War Two.

> Napoleon might be said to have been one of those brilliant, but wild, batsmen who with luck in their favour can hit up a century in record time. In his first innings sixes and boundaries flowed from his bat, but with catches dropped all over the field . . . His luck held for a long time . . . but he never attempted to play for his side and in other features of his game he was quite useless. His second innings was short and ignominious, though the bowling against him was easy and his opponents an unpractised and hastily got together team.[2]

Quite what Corporal Bonaparte himself (let alone the successful opposing general, Wellington) would have made of this, is worth speculation; more recent military leaders, however, have been only too pleased to see themselves as sporting heroes. General Montgomery described his victory at El Alamein in 1942 as 'hitting the enemy for six', while at the end of the Gulf War in January 1990, General 'Stormin' Norman' Schwarzkopf described his final manouevre in the classic American sporting analogy: he was 'making a play'; elsewhere his attacking move was described as a 'Hail Mary play', a well-known football tactic.[3] In each case, it is taken for granted that the audience will immediately decode the metaphor. Sport has here been textualised within a general mode of communication.

However, the classic American fictional form, the Hollywood movie, has found sport very difficult. The insistence on foregrounding only a few major characters makes team sports as hard to deal with comprehensively as war: most Hollywood sports films, like most war films, fall flat on their faces through this basic structural inability. The 1992 drama/documentary *A League of Their Own*, about the women's baseball leagues of the 1940s, proved a pleasant exception, while the three-hour documentary *Hoop Dreams* (1994), a chronicle about three young blacks from disadvantaged homes trying to make it into professional basketball, was at least talked about as an Oscar nomination for 1995. There are, of course, some less insensitive mainstream Hollywood efforts. *Running Man*'s alertness to the dystopian relationship between sport and television was as usual over-individualised around the admittedly impressive figure of Arnold Schwarzenegger. One of *Running Man*'s progenitors, *Rollerball* (1975) is at least one Hollywood sports movie which shows evidence of real thought about the relationship between sports and society – though again it can be read simply as a story of the triumph of 'the individual' over 'the system'. A strong film about a future world in which international sport combines the violence of the circus with the service of a totalitarian state, *Rollerball* portrays an excessively violent form of roller-hockey through the actions of one chief character, the game's greatest player. A handful of films have chosen the rather easier path, displaying their individualistic concerns through the upward and downward paths of boxers: *Raging Bull* and the silly *Rocky* series (1976 on). As was discussed in the opening chapter, that symbol of the 1980s, the worked out male body, was created in part through this discourse – with the founding text the first vehicle to star Schwarzenegger, *Pumping Iron*. This then cascaded into a series of films which pitted men with this

particular version of the male body against the forces of evil
– the Vietnamese (the *Rambo* series), or extra-terrestrials
(*Predator*), or confusingly, cyborgs and humans eventually
uniting against the possibility of machine-made nuclear war
(the *Terminator* films). A sporting film created the heroes
adopted in these more ordinary Hollywood plots.

So the textual presence of sport within discourse is not
restricted to the world of factual, analogic description – or
to the film or television. Throughout the history of the
novel, sporting contests have provided either background
or foreground information through which characters and
events move. The nineteenth-century novelist Anthony
Trollope spent so much of his fictional output describing
fox-hunting (to which he was devoted) that he felt impelled
to apologise for it in his *Autobiography* (1883). Trollope also
described cricket, in one case, in his science fiction novel *The
Fixed Period* (1882), forecasting the use of bowling machines
and specially designed body armour for the players.
(Trollope's invention of sporting cyborgs occurred a hundred years before the emergence of cyberpunk fiction).
Twentieth century fiction has likewise made much of sport,
with the stories and novels of P.G. Wodehouse foremost in
their sympathetic portrayals of the meaning of both participation and observation. Wodehouse, whose later life was in
the United States, wrote with insight as well as humour
about soccer, cricket, boxing, baseball and golf, and the
people who play and watch these games. Allen Guttmann
has found several novels dealing with the meaning of life,
the universe, everything, and baseball.[4]

Sport has also generated a great deal of poetry, much of
which is redolent of the social and historical importance of
sport. Here the Barbadian poet Edward Brathwaite encap-
sulates the history of empire in this description of a small
incident in a cricket match – the crowd's reaction to a
scoring stroke by a West Indian batsman off an England
bowler: 'All over de groun' fellers shaking hands wid each
other/as if was *they* wheelin' de willow/as if was *them* had the
power'.[5] It is hard to imagine a clearer expression of the
importance of the sporting contest in the field of international relations, of imagined community, or of the
implicit gender politics of sport.

Most writing about sport, however, falls far short of this

mark. With sports journalism generally being confined to the reporting of particular contests, there is at least the excuse that the first responsibility of the writer is to give the result, and second to account for it in the most immediate way possible. Only then can the writer reflect on the wider structures of particular sports, their history, ownership and so on. This commitment to the result first, immediate explanation second, long-term reflections third if at all, does not rule out the latter, though they tend to occur at set points in the sporting calendar. At the beginnings and ends of championship seasons or festivals like the Olympics, there will be longer-term reflections: these may also appear during local or national crises in these events.

On the whole, however, even the most reflective journalistic discourse of sport is internal, concerned with the playing of games within the established rules. If a national side is failing consistently, as at the time of writing is the case with English football and cricket sides, there is much expression of anger, hatred and misery, but very little questioning of the idea of national teams. The questions of why there is so much public emotional investment in them, or what is the ideological make-up of current players, are avoided in favour of reflections on skills and abilities – or lack of them. If, as I have suggested, personal and collective motivation is necessary for sports success, and if in England the collective motivation at least has begun to waver, then no amount of tinkering with formations or assertion that skill levels need to be raised will make any difference to the continued long-term decline of this particular postcolonial 'nation'. What is needed is a new set of desires – or a new set of contests which bypass or replace the nation state.

It may be too much to expect television or newspaper journalists who are themselves constructed within an ideology of unreflective patriotism to reflect on it in public. It is not too much to expect such people to be aware of the ethnic and gender politics of the sports they cover, or of their own profession. All too often they are (or seem to be) deeply unaware of them. British television commentators, notoriously, often seem the only people in football crowds who cannot hear any racist chanting. On the other hand, sports journalists, most of whom are men, can see only too clearly the femininity of female performers. They will often comment adversely if they consider female athletes unattractive or 'manly' in appearance. This could be because they are concerned with drugs, and believe drug-takers to be distorting their bodies in the cause of success. It could be that they are unreflectively, or even deliberately, sexist. Whether or not they are doing this deliberately, they are propagating a set of very restricted codes of femininity to an audience of men and women which may well then recognise and internalise those codes. The discourses of sport, like those of fashion and diet, can and do produce and reproduce ideals of the body. They can also produce and normalise ideas of the career, and here too sports reporting can restrict women, or exclude them altogether. There are comparatively few female sports reporters (and very few female coaches). Awareness and articulacy about these forms of sexism as an issue would be welcome.

Again, it may be argued that it is not the job of the sports reporter to change society, or even to reflect continually on its shortcomings. Given that journalism does have severe limits of time and space, it might be hoped that books about sport would be more reflexive and aware of the cultural and historical place of sport. There is very little evidence of this. Leaving aside the limited number of academic studies of sport as a historical phenomenon or cultural practice, many new sports books make their way each year on to the booksellers' shelves. Here there should be space for critical reflection on the place of sport in society.

On the whole, unfortunately, books about sport continue the restricted practices adopted by most newspaper or magazine sports journalism. Take biographies, for example, the most popular form of book-length sporting text. To be sure, most autobiographies or biographies about black sports personalities will contain some reference at least to racism, and in the case of West Indians (and Indians and Pakistanis) usually to the structures of imperialism, and the contemporary politics of sport in the Third World as well. Journalist Dave Hill's biography of footballer John Barnes, *Out of his Skin*, offers

an exemplary chronicle of a sporting life which, whatever
its successes, has been constricted by the continual impact
of racism.[6] Or they may offer insight unobtainable
elsewhere into the work experience of the player. Football
manager Steve Perryman's autobiography *A Man for All
Seasons*, which records his playing career, is an unusually
honest look at the ways in which the structure of the game,
including the coaching staff of one particular club, can
take the enjoyment out of sports performance by coaching
the player not to use or develop his skills, but merely to
perform a restricted role in the team.[7] *Quest for Number
One*, by Robin Smith and John Crace, is another unusually
frank look at the psychological as well as technical
strengths and weaknesses of a cricketer.[8] It was published
as Smith's Test career went into temporary decline, and
the book shows why.

These are notable exceptions. The average sports
biography is actually a hagiography, recounting the great
deeds of a saintly person, with the emphasis on the
statistical rather than the social, or even what there is of
the private life of the subject. These are usually books,
however well written, to read once, quickly, and then to
forget.

One excellent autobiography by a fan should be
mentioned here, partly because of its impact on the world
of polite culture: Nick Hornby's *Fever Pitch* is an insightful
and only ironically celebratory look at the life of a
dedicated soccer fan.[9] Hornby admits to the pain,
boredom, frustration of soccer spectating – all doubled
since he is an Arsenal fan, and even *their* successes are
hardly the cause for national celebration.[10] He notices and
explores the ways in which his infatuation weaves across,
confirms and disrupts relationships with the rest of his
family (especially his father), with friends and lovers. This
frank appraisal of the psychic, domestic and public impact
of fandom was launched at just the right time, two years
after Paul Gascoigne's exquisite skills and tears during the
1990 World Cup Finals had enthralled the chattering
classes and relegitimised the game in the public eye, and as
the fanzine movement tried to re-humanise and repoliti-
cise the soccer spectator. It was also very well written, and
very funny. It was read on radio, turned into a play, and

became part of a New Laddish 1990s masculinity – one of the ways through which middle-class men acknowledged their pain, and even their fidelity. There followed a deluge of books on soccer by journalists and 'writers'.[11] Soccer even crossed over into middle-class musical culture, with Benedict Mason's opera *Playing Away*, an exploration of the Faust legend in which a great player pays his debt to the devil by breaking a leg during his last big match.[12]

The work of Hornby and those who have followed him, 'the soccerati', has provided insight and analysis, mainly of the present and the personal. Further enlightenment might be expected from the histories of sports or particular teams; the more collective focus should give more opportunity for a look at the social conditions of sport. It is seldom delivered. Usually written for a target audience of fans (and implicitly young teenage male fans), histories of teams or events simply catalogue successes and failures, often overwritten as triumphs or disasters. They may well help to form the bond between fan and team which helps to keep the sport in being, but they do little else than provide that sense of the development of the worshipful entity which fans expect. On the whole, controversy is avoided, and the state of being a fan is uncritically celebrated. Many writers, no doubt, are as much fans as Nick Hornby, but lack his expressive gifts; others are responding to the wishes of publishers, who merely wish to reach the target audience of fans and are unconcerned with the place of sport, or sporting literature, in the wider world. Publishers, indeed, seem to think that sporting literature exists in a vacuum, read by those who read nothing else. While there are books which seek to challenge and inform rather than confirm beliefs, the majority do not.

There are, of course, exceptions to this rather depressing rule. The literature of cricket, for example, is one of the most well-developed in the world of sports publishing. As befits a game stretching back in recognisable form to the eighteenth century, cricket has accumulated a distinct literary tradition, one which above all other sports contributes to the ways in which the game has been played as well as read. This is not to say that the literature of cricket avoids the traps. Most books about cricket are written within the hagiographical, the statistical, or the nostalgic tendencies of most sports writing. Lives and careers of great players recount their averages rather than discussing the politics of selection. Histories of the game, whether in Britain or overseas, are usually nostalgic assertions of the unique place played by the sport in national life. In 1993 British Prime Minister John Major shared with a political audience his own nostalgic view of 'shadows lengthening over county grounds' – for him, this is an aspect of eternal and unchanging Englishness (in this case the vision is far from eternal, but dates from the time of the 'invention of tradition'. County grounds are as old as the cricket County Championship, i.e. about one hundred years old).[13] Prime Minister or pork butcher, readers of cricket books expect to find a golden age of demon bowlers, cavalier batsmen and comic umpires: by and large they find them. However, there are enough books which do not fall into this pattern for the alert cricket reader to get the idea that there is life beyond the shadowy county pavilion, and that it interacts with events on the field.

That bible of cricket itself, the annual publication *Wisden Cricketer's Almanack*, is at first sight simply a mass of statistics, detailing batting and bowling feats since time began – even the births and deaths of cricketers are included in an excess of seemingly useless information. In a short section at the beginning, they will also find essays on topics of the moment, and especially the editor's notes – a section which in recent years has been full of upstanding and trenchant comment about the game. It is clear from these notes that cricket is and has always been, to use a common sporting analogy, a 'political football', subject to interactive interference from governments as well as boards of control, and that international relations and movements in the structure of ownership affect the game. Many books on cricket address these issues, the class, ethnic and international politics of the game. David Lemmon's *The Crisis of Captaincy* is a case in point.[14] Lemmon, a full-time journalist and writer on cricket, analyses the English game in the 1980s with reference to the politics of class and post-imperial international relations, seeing an increasingly proletarian captaincy finally taking cricket to the position of professional soccer in the late nineteenth century, in an international scene dominated by political tensions. He is also sensitive to the public desires invested in the role of captain in an age when, he claims, success (including commercial success) is the only yardstick.

The commercialisation of the game is one of the starting points for former Wisden editor Graeme Wright's book *Betrayal: the Struggle for Cricket's Soul*, a survey of cricket's recent past.[15] Since the ending of amateur status in 1963, he reasons, the game has gone to the dogs. Too much cricket is played at too low a standard; the county game will die if it is not rescued from mediocrity, and if it dies, Test cricket will die alongside it. But is the county game worth saving? Wright's account is suffused with a myth which complements John Major's vision of Englishness: 'cricket's soul'. Cricket is still, he argues, a national symbol of decency and fair play. This myth consorts oddly with his account of real players, many of whom cheat, and few of whom give their all, even when playing for their country. Many cricketers, indeed, as he points out, readily forfeited international careers when offered lucrative contracts by Packer or South Africa. Wright argues that if county players are, as he sees it, bored by the game, there must be some return if not to amateur status, then to the involvement of part-time players who could enjoy the game, and communicate their enjoyment.

Wright's book, like Lemmon's, is aware of the politics of class and nation, capital and commerce, and the ways in which they interact with and indeed help to produce the game. Yet the nostalgic tendency is also here (unsurprisingly in an argument about the dangers of modernisation); the book's points are interspersed with recollections of cricketing triumphs and disasters, and reflections on the strengths and otherwise of players and officials, whose prominence in the text sometimes obscures the argument. Anyone brought up to find the golden age in all cricket books will be able to find it here. Hard as he has tried, New Zealander Wright has not been able to work outside the pervasive discourse of cricket writing. London-based American Mike Marqusee, on the other hand, goes straight for the jugular in his study *Anyone But England*.[16]

He mixes admiration for the game with a defiantly recidivist left politics to produce an indictment of British post-imperialism and post-Thatcherism. Cricket here is a register of all the ills of British society. The racism, the misogyny, the continuing politics of class, the over-exploitation of the players, and the commercial greed of the game's administrators, are all shaken up in a stirring account of national decline and consequent neurotic nationalism. Yet like Wright, Marqusee cannot end without invoking the qualities of a game he loves:

> Revival is about more people playing the game, getting more joy out of it, seizing and remaking it for their own purposes, just as the élite seized and remade the peasant game in the eighteenth century. It is about playing the game to a higher standard, a standard not judged by winning or losing, but by degrees of invention and imagination. It is about exploring the limits of the game, and transgressing them.[17]

Cricket-writing in many ways has become a literature of its own. The other main exception to the rule of semi-literate sports writing is the literature of field sports. Repellent as it may seem – and I write as one who disapproves of the torturing and killing of animals – this literature often engages holistically and convincingly with the experience of being in the world; despite (or perhaps because of) its subject it is an ecological literature, from Izaak Walton's classic text *The Compleat Angler* (1653) through poet and landowner Siegfried Sassoon's semi-autobiographical social journal *Memoirs of a Fox-Hunting Man* (1928), or the memoirs of a big-game hunter turning towards the politics of conservation, such as Fred G. Merfield's *Gorillas Were My Neighbours* (1949); in a similar category is another book regarded as a classic text, Ernest Hemingway's reflections on bull-fighting, *Death in the Afternoon*.[18] Hunting here is seen as sport, not as a means of subsistence; as something which gives pleasure, but which also puts the hunter in touch with profound truths about the natural world, the community and the self. There is sometimes a strong sense of imagined community here, but as often a sense of imagined ecology which perhaps in these days of ecocide is more important. It is an absurd paradox that hunting, shooting and fishing require the preservation of traditional landscapes and wildlife populations, however artificially controlled, that would otherwise be destroyed by pesticidal agriculture or property development.

The unofficial discourse of sport has burgeoned in Britain in recent years. The last decade has seen the emergence and consolidation of a football fanzine movement, and the consolidation was helped by the important part the fanzines played in the political resistance to the proposed membership card law. As with any fan culture, the number of fanzines is always fluctuating as the editors and contributors begin with enthusiasm or lose interest, or in the case of some of the more professionally produced magazines, go broke. Although many fanzines are very old-fashioned domestic products, typed and pasted up in a crude fashion, others are confident products of the desk-top publishing revolution.

The football fanzines have influenced the creation of fanzines for other sports: cricket, tennis, golf. One of the principles of this informal or unofficial mode of publication is that anyone can do it. Anyone can make and sell their own magazine, anyone can contribute their views. They are, therefore, unwelcome at some of the venues they are produced for; there are a few cases of legal action taken by clubs against the vendors of magazines. Some football clubs, on the other hand, have taken the presence of the fanzines seriously; at least one club has invited supporters to contribute on a regular full page slot in its official matchday programme, and printed a wide range of submissions, from nostalgia pieces about great teams and players to an attack on racism at football grounds which looked suspiciously like a political tract.

It would be impossible to produce a convincing structuralist reading across hundreds of ephemeral publications, but two of the constant themes of the fanzine discourse have already been noted. They are nostalgic, constantly referring to the teams and players of the past; and they are within limits politically correct, very aware of issues of sexism and racism at football grounds. The limits include a tendency to 'anything goes' humour at the expense of other clubs, especially whoever happens to be the local rival. And they are constantly critical of the present players, managers, owners, pricing policies and so on; truly here is the articulate voice of the average supporter.

Or is it? These publications are put together overwhelmingly by white males in their twenties, who share with their fascination for football (or cricket, golf etc) an interest in independent popular musics of various sorts. Most of them are graduates. For many, the fanzine is a personal strategy, an opening into professional journalism; the number of professionally produced and marketed soccer magazines has increased markedly as the more personally aggressive of these writers have tried to use their love of football to launch writing careers. If they succeed, for all their positional uniformity, it is to be hoped that they become the contextually aware sports journalists that most newspapers, radio and television stations so desperately need.

Meanwhile one trend which is at least implicit in the fanzines must be addressed and teased out further. The fanzines are not necessarily concerned with the future of sport as a commercial entity; they are necessarily concerned with its future as an object of contemplation. The concern, in other words, is with style as much as with statistics: with the shape of the game, with how it could or should be played, and with what makes watching it into such a pleasurable (or unpleasurable) activity. Fans' obsessions start at least because the object of their worship gives them pleasure. In conclusion, we explore the question of the pleasures of sport.

Notes

1. St. Paul's First Letter to the Corinthians; in the Revised Standard edition of *The Bible*, this is Chapter 9, Verses 24-27.

2. Charles D. Head, *Napoleon and Wellington*, 1939, quoted in I. Pears, 'Wellington and Napoleon', in R. Porter, (ed), *Myths of Englishness*, Polity Press, Cambridge pp212-236.

3. C. Carlton, *Going to the Wars*, Routledge, London 1992, p145.

4. Guttmann, *op.cit.*, Chapter 4, 'Why Baseball is our National Game'.

5. T. MacDonald, *Viv Richards*, Sphere, London 1984, p79.

6. D. Hill, *Out of his Skin*, Faber, London 1989.

7. S. Perryman, *A Man for All Seasons*, London, Pelham, 1988.

8. R. Smith and J. Crace, *Quest for Number One*, Boxtree, London, 1992.

9. N. Hornby, *Fever Pitch*, Victor Gollancz, London 1992.

10. See the hostile reaction to Arsenal's 2-Cup season, 1992-3, in *The Independent*, March 22, 1993.

11. A journalistic example, I. Ridley, *Season in the Cold*, Kingswood Press, 1992, and a writer's, I. Hamilton, *Gazza Italia*, Granta Books, Penguin, Harmondsworth 1994.

12. See 'A neat one-two inside the penalty aria', *The Independent*, May 20, 1994.

13. See E. Hobsbawm and E. Ranger, *The Invention of Tradition*, Cambridge University Press, Cambridge 1982.

14. D. Lemmon, *The Crisis of Captaincy: Servant and Master in English Cricket*, Christopher Helm, London 1988; see also M. Marshall, *Gentlemen and Players*, Grafton Books, London 1987.

15. G. Wright, *Betrayal: The Struggle for Cricket's Soul*, H.F. & G. Witherby, 1993.

16. M. Marqusee, *Anyone but England*, Verso, London 1994.

17. Marqusee, *ibid.*, p256.

18. E. Hemingway, *Death in the Afternoon*, Jonathan Cape, London 1932; ed. cited Penguin, Harmondsworth 1966.

7 Pleasures, Problems, Possibilities . . .

In the end, Johann Huizinga's characterisation of the human species as *homo ludens*, the animals who play, illuminates any consideration of sport and leisure more brightly than theories of modernisation. This final chapter argues that if we are to understand sport we must understand, and encourage, its enjoyment. The insights of sociology and history must be joined by an aesthetics of sport.

The new sporting textuality discussed above offers a way of seeing the pleasures of sport. In the personal responses of Hornby *et al* and the fanzine culture, while there is deep awareness of issues of race, gender, sexuality and power, there is very little overview: no sense of the historical evolution of sports, or of the functional or other sociological models which this book has used to understand them. There is instead a welcome stress on sport as pleasure, sport as play, sport as a necessary part of many contemporary lives. This is a world away from the interpretation offered by the Weber-influenced Guttmann, or the Althusserian Jean-Marie Brohm. Sport is, no doubt, a rationalised and bureaucratised system, which both reflects and constructs aspects of the social system (which is why the very wealthy baseball players of the USA are so deeply alienated from their even wealthier employers); but it remains play, and it is still played and watched for pleasure. An aesthetics of sport – a theorised model of the ways in which sports work to transmit pleasure(s) – will help to escape from the limits of those rationalist models.

This discussion started with an emphasis on the importance of desire and the role the imagination plays in the meaning of sport. It ends with a return to the question which should loom large in any question involving desire and fantasy, but a question which disturbs the relationship between language and sport: the question of pleasure. What is it about sport that gives us pleasure, and how if at all can we account for it?

It may be that we can account for very little, because of the inadequacy of language. The crowd is expressive but inarticulate, using a range of communicative sounds beyond words to convey the excitements and frustrations of the sporting contest. Listen to the shouts of triumph at the end of a golf championship, or the roar of the crowd when a wing sprints to the line to score a try. There is a mixture here of the verbal (i.e. recognisable words) and sounds which are organised and recognisable, and which may even have patterns of localised intensity or 'accent', but which are *not* identifiable as words. Such vocalisations are common to sports crowds, and players, all over the world. It is difficult to attribute definite meanings to these inarticulate vocalisations; does this mean we have to abandon the project of discusssing the language of sport? Not entirely.

The question bears directly on one of the most influential approaches to language and the voice within Cultural Studies, an essay by the French critic Roland Barthes. In this essay, 'The Grain of the Voice', Barthes discussed the voice of the singer, arguing that the best singers pay less attention to the words they are singing than to the joy of the physical act of singing itself.[1] The joy is in the way the breath moves through the body, and the production of sound through the series of openings and vibrating parts which comprise the body. He gave examples of the work of two singers. The German Dietrich Fischer-Dieskau uses all his artistry in an attempt to project the meanings of the words he is singing: the lines of the music, and his own physical pleasure in singing, are sacrificed in the cause of clarity of diction. The Swiss-French singer Charles Panzera (Barthes' singing teacher), on the other hand, paid very little attention to expressing the meanings of the words he was singing, giving himself over instead to the joys of the physical activity of singing: producing a specific sound, the grain of the voice, which expresses a state of being outside and beyond language. Barthes called this state *jouissance* ('ecstasy') as opposed to mere *plaisir* ('pleasure'). This ecstasy, for Barthes, comprises a more genuine musicianship than Fischer-Dieskau's careful clarity. The grainier the voice, in this account, the more authentic. We could relate this account to the unverbal utterances of the crowd, as exemplars of this same unverbal ecstatics. Elsewhere in Barthes's writing there is to be found a related opposition between the activities which provide a reassuring reproduction of the *familiar*, and work which shocks us by departing from familiar routines, which *defamiliarises*. Here again the terms *plaisir* (for the usual) and *jouissance* (for the unusual) can be used. The argument as a whole often boils down to a deep suspicion about the role of language in society. In this argument, it seems that words can be pleasurable, but only by transcending common meanings or transcending words altogether can ecstasy be reached.

This argument about the voice owes much to the French postwar reworking of psychoanalysis, which during the 1980s became almost dogmatic within Anglo-American film and literary theory and feminist criticism, and which influenced political theory through the work of Louis Althusser. These theories suggest that the learning of language is a crucial part of the process whereby we become gendered subjects (actual men and women living in actual cultures). Since all cultures are patriarchal, dominated by and run in the interests of men, then any activity which stresses words and their meanings can only reinforce patriarchy. Several French feminist writers have suggested that women should and could only express themselves through sounds which owe nothing to patriarchal language. Julia Kristeva, for example, claimed that the 'symbolic order' of patriarchy, expressed through normal language use, could be subverted through the 'semiotic order' of unorthodox verbal utterance, for instance the poetry of Mallarme.[2] As with Barthes, the voice's authentic expression is denied where ordinary language is the centre of attention: the 'pre-verbal' somehow carries truths which patriarchal language cannot express. These related forms of essentialist humanism (in other words, ideas about what people really are, about their 'essence' and how they can achieve and express it) remain influential within Cultural Studies. They imply at least that the unverbal articulacy of the sports crowd is an authentic expression of *jouissance* (and no doubt the members of a crowd celebrating a baseball home run or a rugby try would agree); they also imply that this 'subversion' of the restrictions of everday langauge is not specifically necessary to, or appropriated by, women, but available to everyone. They also reinforce the idea that sport gives pleasure. How then, if the articulation of this pleasure lies outside language, are we to account for it?

One approach to this type of non-verbal, non-articulable pleasure would be to call it 'sublime'. The theory of the sublime emerged in eighteenth century Europe; it was a rough contemporary of gothic fiction (the work of Ann Radcliffe and Mary Shelley, for example), in which people were abstracted from the safe, known, and rationally comprehensible worlds of western aristocratic family life and were exposed to the ghostly, the exotic, the oriental, and the southern; and to landscapes, as well as people and behaviours, which were unfamiliar, often frightening, and not susceptible to rational use or explanation. The aesthetic of the sublime, as explored by Kant in Germany and Burke in Britain, emphasised the pleasure available from the unfamiliar even in its extreme, terror, including the terror of inhuman landscapes such as mountains. Their vertiginous surfaces became during the nineteenth century the object of serious sporting endeavour; people risked life and limb to enjoy the sublime pleasures and terrors of mountaineering.

Although it is a long way from the alps to the Crystal Palace athletics stadium, it is perfectly possible to characterise aspects of the experience of sporting participation and spectatorship as sublime. Of course for the participant athletes the sublimity of fear forms an important part of the experience: fear of failure, of humiliation, of injury. Consider the high jump competitor who has reached the last round of the contest, and is jumping against one remaining opponent more experienced than herself, with the bar set a centimetre higher than she has ever cleared in competition before. Whatever adrenalin and other chemicals are doing for that competitor's body, there will be an element of fear as she approaches the bar. Much of this fear will be passed to the watching crowd. Unable to affect the event directly, they will nonetheless experience it vicariously, feeling the terror of the approach run, the moment of determination of the jump itself, and then the relief, triumph or devastation as the bar is cleared or displaced. So we can see sporting pleasure, for performer and crowd alike, as potentially sublime.

The sublime experience is an aspect of the non-verbal, irrational which I have ascribed to the experience of sport. In an interesting article on the evolution of the British soccer crowd, Richard Holt has suggested that this collective entity is 'one of the few arenas left where a partial loss of control was permissible, where even the most stolid men let themselves go for a moment'.[3] Here we should think back to the disussion of carnival and popular culture in Chapter Two. The argument implicit in the work of Bakhtin, and quite explicit in the work of Stallybrass and White, and Sennett, is that since the seventeenth century the public sphere has become dominated by the values of a repressed bourgeois respectability. All these critics, and the more positive Elias school of sociology, are agreed that the public expression of emotion, especially for men, became virtually impossible. Substitutes were found. For the middle class, classical concert music became hypercharged with emotion, partly because it provided one of the few available outlets for this expression. However constrained the concert world was within norms of respectable bourgeois behaviour (the audience was expected to sit in silence, giving polite applause at the end, rather than intervening, applauding or encouraging during the performance), emotions otherwise repressed often came to the surface; it was common for people to faint at these events. Similarly for the working class, music hall provided an opportunity for the irrational, the uncontrolled, the carnivalesque outlet of emotion. The sports crowd, as Holt suggests, is an equally important area for the display of emotion – newspaper reports indicate that male hysteria has been evident in football crowds since people started watching the game. (My own experience, including research on televised crowd behaviour, would suggest that the tide of collective male hysteria rose from the early 1960s on, and that the televising of soccer has been a useful index of this increase).

There are some more general points to be made about the crowd and sporting pleasure. The first is the sense of place. The discussion in Chapter Two made some general points about territoriality. In urban spaces, a sense of territoriality, of physical belonging and/or ownership, must be fashioned from unpromising beginnings. Parts of any locality will be owned by individuals, and the collective representatives of local councils and the like; but the administration of large urban areas is depersonalised and subdivided, with different authorities responsible for services such as water, gas and electricity, telecommunications, the collection of rubbish, the maintenance of roads and the provision of public transport, policing, and so on. When most of these were national or municipal organisations, some admittedly vague notion of public ownership was possible. Not any more. Urban spaces are crossed and recrossed by lines of communication which are seen as necessary to public and domestic life, but which belong to others. In this privatised-public world the identification and occupation of common areas is especially important to a sense of place. The village green or the school playing field can fairly easily fulfill this function; in large urban areas the sports stadium provides this vital link precisely because it allows for the congregation of large numbers of people. While we should not forget the potentially negative aspects of strong local identification, it must be emphasised that in an increasingly fragmented public sphere, such large-scale meeting places can fulfil a vital social function. It is important, therefore, that poorer and/or local spectators should not be priced out in the great rebuilding of stadia which has followed the Taylor Report on the Hillsborough disaster. The stadium is and should be an important public space, the space in which the collective experience of the sublime can be felt and expressed.

Whether its expression is constituted through verbal or

non-verbal means, one of the continuing meanings of sport for men in particular is precisely that it addresses the body. In a world where male articulacy sees the male body as an unproblematic whole, it is absent from most discourse. Discussion of the body and its desires are approached, if only obliquely, through the discourses of sport more than anywhere else. The workings of the body, its successes and failures as a machine, are debated in the pages of the sports newspapers and their television equivalents, and in casual discussion, in ways which are not replicated in political or social discourse. While for women this is less important (as many women are only too aware of their bodies as problematic), there are complementary ways in which their ages, shapes and levels of fitness are expressed and controlled through discourses of sport and through sporting activities such as aerobics and related gymnastic activities. How are we to account for the location of the body within the discourses of sport?

Firstly we could stay on the territory of psychoanalysis and relate work on sport to work on the domain of bodily desires and activities on which psychoanalysis has concentrated: sex and sexuality. For most versions of psychoanalysis, whether or not they are principally concerned with the person's entry into language, the problems of early relationships with the body, parents and the world mean that our 'subjectivity' is constituted by a lack. We all feel incomplete, all the time. Humanity is characterised through the constant presence of desire to make good that lack. We 'are' through our wish to become what we are not. Descartes' famous formula about himself, 'I think, therefore I am', would have to be rewritten to 'I want, therefore I will become'. The quest for sporting victory is one common way of expressing this fundamental human feeling.

It is important to notice in this connection that a common attempt to transcribe the experience of sporting achievement involves precisely the feeling of transcending the normal limits of the self. Far from simply expressing physical ecstasy, which in Barthes' model is too simply a product of the body, it is seen as the transcendence of the body and its limits. After becoming the first human to run a mile in less than four minutes, Roger Bannister recalled the moment in childhood when he had realised what running could mean for him, and why he had a burning desire to continue to run: 'I was running anew, and a fresh rhythm entered my body. No longer conscious of my movement, I discovered a new unity with nature'.[4] Paradoxically, many of the 'martial arts' are practised so as to achieve this feeling of unity. Morikei Uyeshiba, the inventor of aikido, developed the sport after a revelatory experience while meditating – he developed it as an active form of meditation. In some forms of aikido, there is no confrontational competition, and the graceful movements of self-defence are practised by the leading practitioners as a form of dance. The Chinese self-defence sport tai chi-ch'uan is also practised as a gymnastic dance by many of its practitioners. The competition rifle shooter Malcolm Cooper, winner of a string of Olympic medals and World Championships, tries to achieve the required state of focused concentration and economy of movement through zen meditation; Arthur Ashe defeated Jimmy Connors at Wimbledon in 1978 through a peak of concentration achieved by meditating between games. Even in competitive sport, then, time and again a successful player describes this feeling of transcendence, often expressed as a feeling that the player is actually observing the performance. In this account sport becomes a way of escaping from the common limits of humanity and the body. The wish to achieve this state is one of the most powerful of the utopian fantasies. It drives many musicians, for instance, and those who attend concerts in order to escape from the everyday; it drives sports performers and those who watch them, for equivalent reasons.

These are, however, moments rarely achieved. The body is more usually celebrated through sporting activity as *apart from*, rather than *a part of*, nature. It is easy to see the importance which this account of human development must give to fantasy and desire; easy also to see how fantasy and desire are commonly focused on sex. The easy identification of sex and desire, however, leads psycho-analysis to insist, all too often, that sexuality is the grounding of all fantasy and desire, and that desires which are directed in other ways are transpositions; what is really being expressed in virtually everything is sexual desire. The implication is that success in any field, including sport, is the expression of sexual desire or frustration, and that sporting achievements such as goalscoring are themselves ritualised re-enactments of sex.[5] It is difficult to argue with such a generalised, reductive view of life, but also difficult to square this approach with the sexualities on display in sport. Promiscuous and celibate, gay and lesbian sportspeople are successful. If goalscoring is a substitute for sex, then why were footballer George Best, or basketball star Magic Johnson, so sexually promiscuous? There is more to fantasy and desire, more to living and becoming, than sexuality. However important the body is in sport, there is more to sporting pleasure and bodily pleasure than sexuality.

Such as what? As well as an insistence on the pleasures of local, regional and national identities which have been a recurrent theme here, what is needed is an aesthetics of sport, which takes account of movement and of interpretation. The great historian C.L.R. James wrote in his classic book *Beyond a Boundary*, 'We may some day be able to answer Tolstoy's exasperated and exasperating question – "what is art?" – but only when we have learnt to integrate our vision of Walcott on the back foot through the covers with the outstretched arm of the Olympic Apollo'.[6] In an extraordinary chapter of his book James argues that the principal reason for the absence of sport from aesthetic theory is that both aesthetics and those who discuss aesthetic theories are elitist and that sports especially as the elite see them, are popular. The elitism prevents people on both sides of the high/mass culture divide from seeing that sports belong in the same domain as theatre, ballet, opera and dance. Individual characters against a background of teams, and the general public whom they represent, stand in conflict with each other and move towards a resolution of the drama.

One constant reference point which links the worlds of sport and art, in fact, is drama. Roland Barthes wrote of wrestling as akin to Greek tragedy in its opposition of good and evil, and of the Tour de France as like the epic poetry of the classical era, in which a long journey by heroes involves confrontation with both themselves and with outside forces. It is almost routine for sports commentators to present individual matches or moments within them as 'dramatic' – there is plentiful use of drama's genres, epic, or comic, or tragic. We can usually see what they mean. But are these metaphors adequate – and even if sports are dramatic, how can this help to explain the pleasures of sport?

Can we simply blanket all sports with the term dramatic? There are some relatively undramatic sporting activities. Personal fitness work such as weight training or jogging, and their collective equivalents such as aerobics, usually lack the elements of conflict and resolution between characters which we associate with the dramatic. Even here, though, the drama may be intense. A confrontation between an unresponsive body and a mind intent on realising a fantasy of personal transformation can be as gripping as any narrative of international conflict on the sportsfield – or the battlefield for that matter. Moving to more public sporting/recreational activities, such as hill walking, fell running and mountaineering, all are clearly dramatic in outline, if not always in realisation: the relationship between the human body and the 'natural' always has the potential for conflict, and is sometimes realised in a 'victory' for the landscape; human death and injury are more commonplace in mountaineering than in any other sporting activity.

Each sport contains the elements of confrontation, crisis and resolution which are necessary to drama. Even the most aestheticised, and least ostentatiously confrontational spectator sports, such as ice dance, are presented within the framework of competition; in 1994 there was a particularly dramatic confrontation between two American skaters. Nancy Kerrigan was assaulted just before the winter Olympics, and it was alleged that an associate of her rival Tonya Harding had carried out the assault. The incident was immediately signed up by Hollywood. Even without such excesses, ice dance, as much as any other sport, carries within it the possibility of dramatic failure occasioned by error (for example, a partner's failure to catch properly, resulting in a twisted ankle) – the kind of eventuality for which commentators often call on the rather overworked term, 'tragedy'.

Yet it may seem absurd to apply the term drama, let alone tragedy, to a brief confrontation on the field of play between millionaires who will not be physically affected by the event, and will presumably repeat the exercise in the near future. Perhaps it is preferable to take a more inclusive view. In most team sports there is a macro-drama, that of the season, which includes with it the mini-dramas of individual matches, and micro-dramas of confrontations between players and/or officials. It is possible, indeed almost routine, for a team to defeat all and sundry for two months at the start of a season, and yet to win nothing at its end. In gladiatorial circus sports likewise there are micro-narratives of injury and loss of form during tournaments, held within a macro-narrative of the global success and failure of the participants on a particular tour in a particular year.

These narratives, however eagerly they are consumed by fans, have only a routinised impact on the public. It could be argued that the really important moments in sport are the great first achievements which seem to open new worlds of human possibility, such as the ascent of Everest by Sherpa Tensing and Edmund Hilary, or the first four minute mile, run by Roger Banister, in the early 1950s (or perhaps the scale of achievements like Martina Navratilova's domination of Wimbledon, or Liverpool Football Club's of the Football League Championship, in the 1980s, which again seem to rewrite the scale of human achievement as a whole). In cases such as Everest or the mile, the drama becomes truly public, as crossover is achieved from the back pages to the front pages of newspapers, and for a time displaces the routine stories of political and economic life.

So sport does indeed have the elements of drama within it. This does not make sport a precise analogue of the theatre, which is sometimes assumed to be the natural home of drama. Whether the dramatic is in the individual confrontation, the gradual unfolding of a championship season, or the arrival of something qualitatively new in the field of sporting achievement, the sense of the dramatic in sport is rather different from that normally experienced in the theatre. Most theatregoers will know the plot of the play they are about to see – it will be outlined in the

programme book even at a première; in many cases
members of the audience will be as familiar with the words
as the cast. The pleasure resides not in the excitements
and moments of suspense of the storyline (real though
they may be) but in the ways in which the actors can
perform. Retelling the known is in most cases refamiliarisation. Most people attending the last day of an open golf
championship, similarly, will know at least most of the plot
(the winner will usually emerge from a small group of
players) but they cannot know in advance its final act; they
will see the drama unfold in real time. This creation of real
time suspense, and its resolution, is one of the great
pleasures of most team sports. Before the match starts, all
present will know the rules, but only when the match is
over will they know its narrative.

The pleasures here, then, are in improvisation. The
analogue is with music; not classical concert music (in
which again the narrative is usually known to the audience
and the pleasure is all in the interpretation of the details of
its realisation), but with jazz (and equivalents such as
Indian classical music), music which contains and
structures improvisation. In jazz, performers and audience will be familiar with the rules, they will be familiar
with the instruments used, and with the types of melody
and harmony, if not with the actual tunes themselves. The
interest lies in the ways in which the players can perform
within those rules, or perhaps through innovation in
technique, or individual or collective insight, actually
transcend the rules. The virtuoso jazz musician can quite
literally perform the impossible (or rather the previously
unthinkable) – but cannot be relied on to do so. Similarly
the great sprinter, golfer or team game player(s) can, on
the right day, perform the unthinkable – or not. Though
much of sport is familiar and routine, there is as in jazz the
constant tendency towards, even the hope and expectation
of, the unfamiliar.

It is worth returning at this point to that opposition
between *plaisir* and *jouissance* discussed in Barthes' essay
'The Grain of the Voice'. Applying this model to sports, it
could be argued that *plaisir* would apply to a performance
in which victory was achieved through the methodical
application of the rules, team discipline where necessary,

and so on. There is pleasure, *plaisir*, in the familiar. Where, on the other hand, victory was achieved through greater than normal skill, or innovation which is not contradicted by the rules, *jouissance* might be derived. There is pleasure, *jouissance*, in the unfamiliar. Refamiliarisation and defamiliarisation are both available through sport – though as I say the constant scope for improvisation means that there is a stronger tendency towards the latter than in some forms of western art.

It's neat – too neat to fit. The wild card in most sports is the extent, the quality of opposition. The analogy with jazz breaks down here (though there have been 'contests' between bands, or drummers, or tenor sax players, these are abnormal, whereas confrontation is routine in sport). This makes the search for the unfamiliar all the more vital, as opponents will have trained to be prepared against each others' known routines – so even the routine may be impossible if opponents' routines work, and your team's counter-tactics don't. So because of the quasi-improvisatory and confrontational nature of almost all sporting activity, room firstly has to be made for luck (e.g. an opponent, in the team leading into the final leg of a relay race, who drops a baton at the handover; or an injury which allows a young player into the team – who goes on to score the game's winning try). Luck of this sort could be said to be a form of defamiliarisation – certainly it can make both participants and observers very happy.

Secondly, we have to have some notion of degree. A winning goal scored by a toe-poke from two yards after a series of miskicks, but in the last minute of a cup final, is going to produce a more *jouissant* reaction among scorer, team mates and spectators alike than one scored from a perfect shot after a wonderful display of precision passing, but which occurs half-way through the second half of a February mid-table contest, and which reduces the score deficit from four-nil to four-one. However defamiliarising, such a goal may not even register on the players' or supporters' *plaisir* scale if the opposing team happens to be particular local rivals.

There is thirdly, then, the question of defeat. Are the pleasures of sport always derived from victory, or skills harnessed in the achievement of victory? Can the formula 'it is better to take part than to succeed' have any validity in a world which values success, in which stardom and sponsorship flow from victory and nothing from defeat? Well, yes, actually. Clearly many participants enter sporting competitions knowing that they are not going to win. Roughly 6,000 of the participants in any Olympiad will be unrewarded with medals. Some will be close; others unlucky; many, however, will be happy to represent themselves and their countries whatever the result. They will be happy to take part; and in tennis, golf, and cycling, there are large numbers of professional competitors who make up the field, but who have very little chance of victory. While this attitude might not apply to the leading professional sportspeople taking part in prestigious tournaments, there are occasions when players receive large amounts of 'appearance money', and in which for that reason the taking part becomes at least as important as the winning.

Towards the end of the 1987 cricket season the MCC celebrated its bicentenary by staging a cricket match which opposed teams representing the English county game and the rest of the world. Appearance money was generous; the match was televised, and also received the courtesy of ball-by-ball coverage on radio. As Graeme Wright wrote in the following year's *Wisden Cricketer's Almanack* (and pointed out later in his book *Betrayal*), the resulting contest was entertaining, indeed thrilling, as the world's best players showed their skills in an atmosphere which lacked the fierce competitive edge of the Test match, so often too aggressively tense to be pleasurable. All who took part agreed that it had been an occasion worth repeating. It hasn't been repeated; instead, any number of mickey mouse one day competitions have appeared, all of which use the same tired oppositions of nationalities; in which there remain the usual possibilities of victory, defeat, and the chauvinisms which surround them.

To face that question more honestly. Are the pleasures of sport available in defeat? For the spectator, undoubtedly so unless her favourite(s) perform without any distinction. For participants, at any level, it is rare for the admission of pleasurable defeat – though it does happen. For the unpleasantly defeated, there remains the undiluted negative of pleasure, the tragic. If most games, most championship seasons in most sports, are in essence dramas, then most are in some sense 'tragedies' for the defeated. Or rather, in most sports defeat gives us the opportunity to consider the meaning of tragedy, as it impacts on individuals such as performers and on groups such as their supporters.

This is a somewhat luxurious position; perhaps, again, a dangerously self-indulgent use of the word tragedy. There are real human tragedies in sport: some forty people lost their lives while climbing or walking in the Scottish mountains during the winter of 1993–4; boxers and rugby players often emerge from contests scarred, paralysed, and each year a few die. Sporting tragedies are often very public, especially when they happen to world stars: for example, the death of Ayrton Senna, or the gradual descent of the once joyously articulate Muhammad Ali. But human death and disfigurement remain comparatively rare; the constant presence of death, the real tragedy in sport, is in the murder of animals, the closest we come today to the Roman carnival of carnage. In Ernest Hemingway's words:

> The bullfight is not a sport in the Anglo-Saxon sense of the word, that is, it is not an equal contest or an attempt at an equal contest between a bull and a man. Rather, it is a tragedy; the death of the bull, which is played, more or less well, by the bull and the man involved and in which there is danger for the man but certain death for the bull.[8]

Yet Hemingway insists that this essential and everyday confrontation with the tragedy of death is not the only focus of the meaning of the bullfight. For him, its movements form a living sculpture; indeed, he remarks at one point, 'I know of no modern sculpture . . . that is in any way the equal of the sculpture of modern bullfighting'.[9] His favourite matador, the gypsy Cazancho,

> moves the cape spread full as the pulling jib of a yacht before the bull's muzzle so slowly that the art of bullfighting, which is only kept from being one of the

major arts because it is impermanent, in the arrogant
slowness of his veronica becomes, for the seeming
minutes that they endure, permanent.[10]

This is precisely the point which C.L.R. James is trying to
make when he asks us to integrate our vision of the great
scoring stroke in cricket with great sculpture; and precisely
the point I was trying to make when I compared the
drama of sport to that of jazz. Both sport and jazz share
this element of moving, of improvisation, an element
which pulls against the rationalised and bureaucratised
view of aesthetics which has dominated the criticism of the
arts, as well as sport, in the West since the Renaissance. As
we saw in Chapter Two, one of the most influential
analyses of sport, Allen Guttmann's, fits the modern
sporting world into this model. As we also saw, it doesn't,
actually, quite fit. Neither, happily, does most art,
although the fixed arts can at least be approached through
rationalist systems of formal analysis. Formalism and
improvisation, however, indeed formalism and *jouissance*,
are not the best of companions. Hopefully my examination of Guttmann's Weberian version of sport will have
indicated some of the problems of this approach, which in
the supra-rational, statistical approach of 'the sporting
record' reaches extremes of abstraction not matched in
criticism of the arts (save perhaps in the mathematical
excesses of musical analysis). In the end the arts, and
sport, are not reducible to their statistical components.

   While most would accept that this is the case (few critics
of the work of Michelangelo bother to calculate the
amount of each pigment, or the number of upward as
opposed to sideways brushstrokes, used in the painting of
the ceiling of the Sistine Chapel), there remains the
problem of impermanence; or does there? In the age of
mechanical reproduction, even 'impermanence' can be
recorded and preserved. To return to the musical analogy:
much jazz improvisation may be impermanent; but so
much has been recorded that one of the problems in
recent jazz is that it has become over-historicised; young
players reproduce older players' styles and techniques, to
the detriment of any originality of which they are capable.
Thanks to recording, jazz is not, actually, impermanent.

Similarly, while many – the vast majority – of sporting events are lost as soon as the performers' legs stop running, sport as a body of techniques and styles, of bodily movements, are a matter of permanent record. Most sport played professionally is televised at some level. Somewhere in the world.

While, as Chapter Three mentioned, the televising of most sport is technically primitive and an inadequate reflection of the 'whole game', and while a few sports such as squash are virtually untelevisable, most popular sports are permanently available in the form of video recording. There are histories (of clubs, seasons, tournaments, players); reviews of sporting years; guides to techniques for every sporting activity from personal/recreational sports like coarse fishing or hang-gliding to detailed guides to positional, defensive or attacking play in team sports; there are guides to officiating; there is a sporting comedy of errors, ('great' goalkeeping errors, rally car crashes, and the like) and there is what could be called a 'sporting pornography' of foul play, the subversion of officials and rules, even of injuries.

Whatever the ostensible reasons for its availability, this permanent record can be studied as a body of aesthetic material as well as a series of techniques, or a narrative of the development of teams or players. Detailed work can be done on the elucidation of this problem, and the search for an adequately descriptive and analytical language for the aesthetics of sport; and it should be done soon, preferably in CD-ROM form; a book is not the place for such an enterprise, which requires the analysis and demonstration of movement.

There are already available models for an aestheticisation of sport and the body; one that would be more widely known were it not for its political associations. The use of the bullfight as an example of sculpture in motion, or anything else, will no doubt be controversial; here's another one. Leni Riefenstahl made an extraordinary film of Adolf Hitler's 1932 election campaign. *Triomph des Willens* is a documentary record made without voiceover (but with added music) which dramatises Lance-corporal Hitler's use of the traditional, the modern, and the populist – a film so successful that Hitler's rival in butchery, the Soviet dictator Josef Stalin, commissioned a remake, with himself as himself/Hitler, and a cast of thousands of actors playing the crowds (who in Riefenstahl's film are actually members of the public). She was then commissioned to produce a film record of the 1936 Berlin Olympics. The result, again, was extraordinary. The film used a number of innovative techniques – for example, trenches were dug alongside long jump and triple jump sandpits, in order for the camera to view the athletes from below. Throughout the film, the body is seen as, precisely, a mobile sculpture. Its very first image, of a naked hammer thrower gradually uncoiling from his immobile starting position, illustrates precisely the way of seeing the body in motion which James requests in *Beyond a Boundary*. It is an image which has been copied recently in British television, in an advertisement for a mobile telephone system (with the typical absence in British television, of the genitals, which are morphed out; the castration of this image also says something about the need for an aestheticisation of the male body. All of it.)

Hopefully a direct comparison between a film made for the Nazi regime, an advertisement for a paradigm of contemporary service capitalism, and an argument put forward by a black West Indian Trotskyist, will have illustrated the difficulty of dismissing Riefenstahl's work or similar visions of the body as 'body fascism'. But the glib phrase seems to have stuck in the current vocabulary of criticism of the worlds of sport, fashion and film. Of course we should beware of aestheticising one particular type of body, as both the Nazis and their Soviet counterparts did. And anyway, even if we do, it won't work: the shape of the body changes. Jesse Owens, the black American who dominated the sprints and long jump at the 1936 Olympics, to the annoyance of the Nazis, and Carl Lewis, the black American who did the same at the 1988 Olympics in Seoul, to more general approbation, look very physically different; the Schwarzenegger effect has ensured that the ideal body for the contemporary male athlete is more muscular, whatever the actual event for which the athlete has trained (in the case of women, the differences are at present less noticeable; Florence

Joyner-Griffith looked far more like her role model, the sprinter and jumper Wilma Rudolph, than Lewis looked like Owens). We may worship an ideal body, but the ideal is unstable, and given the potential in medical technologies, this instability will undoubtedly continue. I hereby cordially invite all those who are uncomfortable with this model to produce a better one.

In the meanwhile, and in the regrettable absence of moving pictures, here are some pointers to a comprehensive sports aesthetic.

What is needed above all else is an aesthetics of unpredictability, one which values and encourages the unfamiliar. Though the task is more difficult than the appreciation of relatively fixed forms such as sculpture, or classical music, this is is not asking the impossible. Jazz improvisation has been modelled and analysed in some detail, and this work could be drawn on in reference to sport's rule-bound unpredictability. Sporting improvisation and defamiliarisation are in fact already, and constantly, the subject of the analysis and commentary through which the media seek to understand and re-present sport: this often involves an appreciation of the unusual. If this type of usually instant consideration is only scratching at the surface, then let us go deeper and quantify the sporting event. Of course this is already done. What I mean is absolutely not quantification in the resolutely descriptive way in which Guttmann's bureaucrats and anorak-wearing statisticians record sport through figures. Contemporary mathematics, through modelling procedures such as catastrophe theory, with its three-dimensional graphs of events; or chaos theory's massive models of change in global ecological systems; perhaps also the more sophisticated wargame programmes; all these could approach the variables and unpredictabilities of sport in such a way as to provide the basis for a more informed analysis and appreciation, even a prediction, of the unfamilar and the unpredictable.

Within this general approach, several specific sources of aesthetic pleasure would need to be modelled.

First, there is the general question of movement. Sports are to be compared, as James and Hemingway say, with painting and sculpture: the lines, curves and motions of the plastic arts are represented in sport in fluid, mobile form. Fluid movements are a major point of attraction in any sporting activity; the darting lines of the fencing contest, the smoothness of the trained golf swing, the slow curve of the cape of Hemingway's matador, are all particular examples of that general rule. A common point of comparison here is with dance; some have argued that team sports are a masculinised and proletarianised version of the ballet. Certainly the lives of the top athlete and the top dancer are similar. In each case recruitment is from a very wide field of hopefuls, very few of whom become professionals. Both dancers and (in most categories) athletes have short-term prime careers characterised by intense physical preparation for comparatively short periods on public display; both are vulnerable to injury in performance or training, and both are vulnerable, through injury, to physical damage which will affect later life (an astonishing number of dancers become seriously arthritic).

There are important differences, apart from the competitive edge which characterise sport, and the improvisatory element of team sports (most dance consists of very strict, learned routines). Women are involved in dance at all levels, as dancers, teachers, administrators and choreographers. Dance is, therefore, a 'feminised' activity in ways which sports, including competitions among women, are not. There are acute dangers of essentialism here, so I should make it clear that by 'feminised' I do not mean that there is some set of characteristics which are 'naturally' female, but that there are some characteristics which, in western societies at least, are associated with women, and which are often valued and practised by them (these characteristics would include for example notions of grace and beauty in movement, or non-competitive co-operation in teamwork). Dance still involves fitness, trained musculature and hard physical work, but it allows the use of the trained body in ways which are not constricted by the immediacy and tension of the sporting goal. We could characterise the body language of sport as improvisatory but because of its goals, as monological, and that of dance as choreographed but dialogical. Because of these differences, including its feminisation, the culture of dance proposes a very different form of masculinity. This is not, as rumour would have it, exclusively gay (indeed some radical gay dance, as performed by a group such as DV8 Physical Theatre, sets itself to explore the more aggressive and competitive sides of masculinity), but it is open to a feminised culture of co-operation which works very differently from the mutually aggressive team spirit of competitive sport – and which is closer to that of feminised team sports like synchronised swimming and (paired and solo) ice dance.

Secondly, a very important aspect of movement, in both the feminised ice dance and the hyper-masculine Australian Rules football alike (and everything in between), is geometry: the movement of bodies and associated sports equipment in space. The rationalisation of sports which produced the limits of space and time of stadium sports enhanced the aesthetic possibilities of geometric interaction. The physical limits of the enclosed space of the playing area make the incisive pass which defeats a defence, the throw to run a player out, or the precisely played hit out of reach of the catchers in the field, all the more impressive. The same limits also increase the excitement caused by the movement of players, for example the blind-side run into space in order to receive that anticipated incisive pass. These are pleasures alike for the observer and performer – pleasures which would be lessened if the games were played in more open areas. Though there are undoubted pleasures in the participation in or observation of field sports – reprehensible though the outcome may be, the sight of a hunt going to work on a frosty winter morning is warming even for those who have not partaken of the customary stirrup cup.

Thirdly, that sight will involve an appreciation of colour in motion. We recognise and appreciate that geometrical movement partly because of the moving pattern of colours across the field. The constant movement of colours against the green and brown of the sporting arena's playing surface, in horse racing the jockeys' silks against the horses' plain or dappled colours, or even the coloured balls moving against the baize on the snooker table, are also purveyors of pleasure in both senses (refamiliarisation and defamiliarisation) used by Barthes. Much of the success of sport on television has been associated with colour in motion; snooker, in particular, would still be a glorified pub game had it not been for the introduction of colour television in the late 1960s. There are no doubt times when the clash of colours is regretted: many Arsenal supporters were disappointed with a recent away shirt; the introduction of baseball (or 'pyjama-style') clothing into English Sunday League cricket has met with almost universal disapproval.

The appreciation of geometric pattern and colour in motion raise, if obliquely, another general question: the question of style. In addition to the pleasures of movement and colour as a general rule, sports observers, journalists and sportsplayers are all aware of the further quality of style. It is a surprisingly controversial issue. In virtually all sports, the movement of some players is especially graceful, where that of others may be powerfully, or brutally effective. In almost all, the question of style versus efficiency is a matter of debate. It may be difficult to pole vault ungracefully, but in most sports there is plenty of room for the merely efficient. Even in boxing, there are some who are characterised as stylists, usually known as 'boxers' (for example, Chris Eubank) to distinguish them from the more brutally effective 'punchers' (Mike Tyson). What is in debate is not whether or not there are graceful and pleasing ways of running, or hitting a ball (or even hitting another person), but whether or not these are more effective than the brutal ways. The short passing game versus the long kick to the centre forward in soccer; the running versus the kicking game in rugby; the caress versus the bludgeon in cricket; all are in debate. What is (usually) unspoken in these debates is another, arguably more important question: the acceptable level of rule-bending, aggressive violence against opponents. At the time of writing there was growing concern at the level of injuries in American football. Despite (or perhaps because of) the comparatively high level of protection given to the players by their body armour and helmets, the kamikaze fierceness of tackling is producing more serious back and neck injuries. There are proposals for new rules to punish illegal tackles more severely.

The dialogue about style and acceptable violence is sparked off by particular incidents. It has always been accepted that the long-ball game in soccer encourages continuous clashes between forwards and defenders. Injury often results. One such incident, in which the then Wimbledon forward John Fashanu jumped for the ball with his elbows flailing in his opponent's face, caused Tottenham Hotspur defender Gary Mabbutt to miss much of season 1993-4 with a fractured cheekbone and eye socket. There followed an intense debate about style and violence, in which those who came to Fashanu's defence argued that the English game has national characteristics of competitive aggression, and a national masculinity was mapped onto these characteristics; the phrase 'it's a man's game' was heard in apparent explanation of this form of cheating. Legal action was threatened over the issue, to the intense embarrassment of the sport's governing body in England, the Football Association. It is at present clear that successful soccer in England and Scotland is a fast and aggressive game, which has an aesthetic of controlled violence; whereas soccer success at European club and international level depends more on patience, skill and subtlety. British clubs competing in European tournaments have recently found to their cost that pace and aggression are no longer enough to win competitions.

Similar differences of aesthetic and practice exist in rugby union. Again, the kicking game in rugby union encourages the over-use of the forwards, and their basic practice of trying to knock or push each other over (a game in which most scoring will be by penalty kicks), at the expense of the backs who like to run with the ball or pass it, and in which much of the scoring will be through tries. Commenting on this tendency, the former England international forward Mickey Skinner claimed that the forward game was the real man's game, while the back row were a bunch of 'Jessicas'; he clearly did not intend the remark as a compliment. Nevertheless, the England coaching staff were at the time of writing claiming without much supporting evidence that they were trying to persuade their players to run with and pass the ball.

Coaches and managers can make a real difference to any game's aesthetic effect. But no-one can make a beautiful game from rules which encourage brutality. In some cases the authorities ruling the game make attempts to intervene on the side of what are considered to be the more aesthetically pleasing as well as the more entertaining sides of their sports. Soccer's rules, which were revised before the 1994 World Cup finals in an attempt to convince American watchers of the beauties of the game by controlling its brutalities, have made it harder for defenders to hurt opposing forwards. The rules of rugby union are reworked on an annual basis in a continuing quest (again directed at positive coverage of the showcase World Cup competition) to encourage, and reward, open, running play.

One current aesthetic debate in cricket concerns the weight of the bat. Cricket bats have to be a regulation size and shape, but can differ in weight by as much as two pounds. Heavy bats will make the ball go further with less effort; lighter bats are easier to control and allow more delicate, precisely placed shots. These are doubtless important questions about the beauties of the game; cricket's debates about violence concern another matter, the question of acceptable levels of intimidation by bowlers. While the weight of the cricket bat does not affect opponents physically, the type of bowling does: short-pitched, fast bowling intended to intimidate has been part of cricket since overarm bowling was legalised; in the 1930s it was the cause of a severe diplomatic incident between Australia and England, and is the cause of continuing and bitter dispute between West Indies and the rest of the cricketing world. Style is part of the argument here, as well as personal safety. It is argued that crowds go to see batsmen play big innings, not duck and weave – or bleed. It is not in dispute that the sight of a fast bowler running in is exciting – and that the very best of these bowlers, like the Australian Dennis Lillee and the West Indian Michael Holding, are graceful as well as exciting to watch. Yet the relief in the cricket world which greeted the arrival of a truly effective slow bowler, the Australian leg spinner Shane Warne, was palpable (especially since the best leg spinner of the previous generation, the Pakistani Abdul Quadir, had recently retired). Here too there is the beauty of the ball in flight, and the unpredictability as it hits the pitch and spins – in either direction – or carries straight on, to the consternation of the batsman in either case. There is general agreement that Warne's success has restored a beauty to the game of cricket which had increasingly been found wanting.

There remain keenly contested debates over whether some activities are sports at all. Ice dance, ski dance and synchronised swimming, eurythmics and other forms of mass gymnastic display, have all been characterised as non-sports by those, mainly men, whose view of sport involves controlled, assertive aggression if not outright violence. Certainly in the case of ice dance (for all the competitive aggression clearly signalled by the Kerrigan incident), the connection with that aspect of the international entertainment circus which does not involve competition is clear: many ice dance winners have gone on to lucrative careers as display dancers in spectacular pantomime shows like 'holiday on ice'. The limited entry of synchronised swimming into the Olympics as a 'display sport' only, and the continuing controversy over the possible entry of competitive aerobics, indicates that the (mainly male) International Olympic Committee is disturbed at the possible blurring of its highly competitive roster of events.

Many other men have no wish to see these boundaries blurred further. When in 1992 the British television station Channel Four showed a series of soccer matches from the English women's league, there was a flood of complaints, and a spirited public debate ensued about the nature of the product. Once again the aesthetics of the game were quite openly gendered. Many men were critical, saying that the women were simply not good enough; when pressed, their views became more explicitly conservative. As well as the predictable opinions that soccer was a 'man's game', and that 'real men' compete 'hard' (so as to hurt each other), even that women have no place in sport and should get back to the kitchen, there was also the slightly more argued position that women were skilled at the technical basics of the game – trapping the ball, passing, shooting, running intelligently off the ball – in much the way men were, but were not physically aggressive or quick enough. British men make exactly the same criticism of soccer from elsewhere in Europe, in Latin America, and especially from Africa.

It seems, then, that even in 1992, the year of the creation of the European Union, the game developed in Britain was perceived to be at the centre of a particular set of *masculine* national characteristics. It might seem daft to call this an aesthetic; but it is, an aesthetic of acceptable violence, comparable in many ways to the acceptable and pleasurable violence argued for by the proponents of a 'safe' consensual sado-masochistic sex. This view of the game is still, I would argue, centred on pleasure – a particular, perhaps regrettable, take on pleasure no doubt, but pleasure none the less.

Is it possible (or even desirable) to offset this brutalised British sporting masculinity? How might this be done? The positive presentation and analysis of all sports as aestheticised spectacle, as stylised geometric movement, rather than national, local or gladiatorial confrontation, would be perfectly possible – if only at the expense of the place-identity which remains an important constituent of sporting pleasure. Whether more would be gained than lost from such a mode of interpretation, given the continued internationalisation of sport some new way of seeing it, one which directly addresses its pleasures, is vital.

To return to that last afternoon of the golfing championship. All the ingredients of contest-based drama and individual achievement are potentially present. But for the spectator, the experience, and the pleasures involved in the assessment of the contest, will be very different if she or he has only attended for the afternoon, or has attended the whole tournament; or followed some or all of it from the television; or has never been to a professional golf tournament before; or does or does not play golf. Different pleasures are available given these different variables and their possible combinations. The drama(s) of the tournament itself will be read differently according to the spectator's experience; it is entirely possible that what is unfamiliar-*jouissance* for one will be familiar-*plaisir* to another, and neither to one who considers herself to be a connoisseur who has seen it all, and seen it done better, many times before. As I said in the opening section of the book, history, memory, fantasy and desire are deeply individualised properties.

But if this is no time to collapse the equally deeply differentiated experiences available through contact with sport into a single set of complementary attributes (or even binary opposites, as I suspect Roland Barthes intended them to be), then the temptation to relativise the individual experience and interpretative skills of participant or spectator/consumer must be resisted. Ah yes, the consumer. As John Hargreaves has argued, sport remains at the apex of capital's work on the body, and consumption, too is a pleasurable activity.[11] Both the act of consumption itself and the preparation for that act (the choices leading to it: shopping, to put it in a nutshell) can be characterised as pleasurable; and here we have the benefit of a wide-ranging group of theoretical discussions on the pleasures of shopping and associated activities.[12]

There is a tendency in all this to chime in with those who have agreed to end history. Nothing matters, so let those of us who can, eat cake. This tendency should be resisted. Since (whatever the more optimistic fantasists of postmodernity might think) capital does not remain static, that means change; not just fashionable change, but linear change. Bodies change according to fashion, no doubt, but longevity and the ageing of the western population are not fashions, but linear changes in the constitution of society, with profound implications for its future – including the future of the body, and therefore the future of sport. Whatever model of the unpredictable we choose, our appreciation and criticism of sport will have to take cognisance of the potential futures of the body, or it will fail to keep up with the field.

Notes

1. R. Barthes, 'The Grain of the Voice', in S. Heath (ed), *Image-Music-Text*, Fontana, London 1977.

2. See the commentary in R. Coward, *Female Desire*, Paladin Books, London 1984, and T. Moi, *Sexual/Textual Politics: Feminist Literary Theory*, Methuen, London 1985.

3. R. Holt, 'Football and the Urban way of Life in Nineteenth Century Britain', in J.A. Mangan (ed), *Pleasure, Profit and Proselytism: British Culture and Sport at Home and Abroad 1700-1914*, Frank Cass, London 1988, p81.

4. Guttmann, *op.cit.*, London, p1.

5. See e.g. G. Vinnai, *Football Mania: The Mass Psychology of Football*, Ocean Books, 1973.

6. James, *op.cit.*, p206.

7. G. Wright, 'Editor's Notes', *Wisden Cricketers' Almanack 1988*, John Wisden and Co., 1988, pp40-41.

8. Hemingway, *op.cit.*, p26.

9. *Ibid.*, p95.

10. *Ibid.*, p17.

11. John Hargreaves, *op.cit.*, p15.

12. D. Miller (ed), *Acknowledging Consumption*, Routledge, London 1995; M. Nava, A. Blake *et al* (eds), *Buy this Book: Studies in Advertising and Consumption*, Routledge, London 1996.

Select Bibliography

This is not a comprehensive guide to my sources, which will be found in the notes, but a selection giving a broad coverage of different areas. Only the edition used has been cited; place of publication is London unless otherwise indicated.

Bale, J. *Sport and Place. A Geography of Sport in England, Scotland and Wales*, R. Hurst 1982.

Beckles, H. McD. *Liberation Cricket. West Indies Cricket Culture*, Manchester University Press, Manchester 1995.

Blue, A. *Grace Under Pressure. The Emergence of Women in Sport*, Sidgwick and Jackson 1987.

Brailsford, D. *Sport, Time and Society. The British at Play*, Routledge 1991.

Brohm, J-M. *Sport, a Prison of Measured Time*, trans I. Fraser, Inter-Links 1978.

Buford, B. *Among the Thugs*, Secker & Warburg 1990.

Carter D., Carter M., and Uzell, D.L. *Football in its Place: An Environmental Psychology of Football Grounds*, Routledge 1989.

Cashman, R. *Patrons, Players and the Crowd: The Phenomenon of Indian Cricket*, Orient Longman, New Delhi 1980.

Cashmore, E. *Making Sense of Sport*, Routledge 1990.

Coghlan, J.F. and Webb, I.M. *Sport and British Politics since 1960*, Falmer Press 1990.

Dunning, E. and Elias, N. *The Quest for Excitement: Sport and Leisure in the Civilising Process*, Blackwell, Oxford 1986.

Dunning, E. and Rojak, C. (eds), *Sport and Leisure in the Civilising Process*, Routledge 1992.

Dyer, K.F. *Catching up the Men: Women in Sport*, Junction Books 1982.

Guttmann, A. *From Ritual to Record: The Nature of Modern Sports*, Columbia University Press, New York 1978.

Hargreaves, John, *Sport, Power and Culture: A Social and Historical Analysis of Popular Sports in Britain*, Polity Press, Cambridge 1986.

Hargreaves, Jennifer. *Sporting Females: Critical Issues in the History and Sociology of Women's Sports*, Routledge 1994.

Hemingway, E. *Death in the Afternoon*, Penguin, Harmondsworth 1966.

Holt, R. *Sport and the British: A Modern History*, Oxford University Press 1989.

Holt, R. *Sport and Society in Modern France*, Macmillan 1981.

Houlihan, B. *The Government and Politics of Sport*, Routledge 1991.

Jarvie, G. and Maguire, J. *Sport and Leisure in Social Thought*, Routledge 1994.

Keller, H. *Music, Closed Societies and Football*, Toccata, 1986.

Kyle, D.G. and Stark, G.D. (eds), *Essays on Sport History and Sport Mythology*, Texas University Press, Austin 1990.

Mangan, J.A. (ed), *Pleasure, Profit and Proselytism: British Culture and Sport at Home and Abroad 1700–1914*, Frank Cass 1988.

Mangan, J.A. and Baker, W. (eds), *Sport in Africa: Essays in Social History*, Africana Publishing, 1987).

Mangan, J.A. and Park, R. (eds), *From 'Fair Sex' to Feminism: Sport and the Socialization of Women in the Industrial and Post-Industrial Eras*, Frank Cass 1987.

Marqusee, M. *Anyone but England: Cricket and the National Malaise*, Verso 1994.

Mason, T. *Sport in Britain*, Faber 1988.

Munsche, P.B. *Gentlemen and Poachers: The English Game Laws 1671–1831*, Cambridge University Press, Cambridge 1981.

Richards, B. *Disciplines of Delight: The Psychoanalysis of Popular Culture*, Free Association Books 1994.

Sutherland, D. *The Mad Hatters: Great Sporting Eccentrics of the Nineteenth Century*, Robert Hale 1987.

Vamplew, W. *Pay up and Play the Game: Professional Sport in Britain 1875–1914*, Cambridge University Press, Cambridge 1988.

Whannel, G. *Fields in Vision: Television Sport and Cultural Transformation*, Routledge 1992.

Wright, G. *Betrayal: The Struggle for Cricket's Soul*, Witherby 1993.

Index